David Kamp

# HEALING GARDEN

images
Publishing

# CONTENTS

# PREFACE

I believe design is an expression of values. And within the designed environment—through the places we build to play, live, work, learn, and heal—we express our hopes and aspirations.

We must remember we are ourselves a product of nature. So, over the course of hundreds of thousands of years our evolutionary development, and eventually our cultural advancement, has been the result of endless interactions and adaptive responses to the natural environment. Even our cultural aspirations were functionally and poetically linked with nature. However, in recent centuries that dynamic changed as technology and science gave us the opportunity to transform ever-greater parts of the natural world. Seen as a pendulum, the world's cultures have been swinging towards reducing direct connections to nature, so that today some people even question the need to include nature in anything but as a source of technological advancement and sustenance. As the world is now becoming so urbanized, direct personal and community responses to nature are becoming marginalized.

Happily, as the projects represented in this book will show, the pendulum is returning to a more inclusive attitude toward nature. Urban historian Sam Bass Warner calls it 'rediscovering a common wisdom' while social ecologist Stephen Kellert eloquently says it is our birthright. This is what world famous biologist E. O. Wilson describes as Biophilia, 'the urge to affiliate with other forms of life.' It is a core realization that there is a fundamental link between humans and nature.

Probably nowhere are the need for a connection to nature more poignant than in times of illness and crisis, where balance and continuity are threatened, and our sense of isolation and vulnerability heightened. A growing body of research is confirming that a connection with nature is essential to health and well-being. This benefit manifests in many ways, including reducing stress and depression, encouraging exercise and social connections, and accelerating healing with less medication.

Such a shift in attitude and perspective demands a design response that is sensitive, adaptive, creative—in short, holistic. It requires us to reflect on the historical and cultural underpinnings of the art and science of healing as we embrace a future of dramatic and complex change—in climate, resources, and a multitude of other forces. It also requires that we practice design as a social art, with dialogue and in collaboration.

Any complex, designed environment requires collaboration between designers and specialists who can articulate both conceptual concerns and the myriad details that must be addressed if a project is to succeed. Several of the most exciting developments underway are collaborative research projects connecting design and health. The benefits of such collaborations are being recognized in a variety of settings—from established health-care environments, such as hospitals and assisted living facilities, to the larger environment including specialized gardens in park settings, healthy neighborhoods and communities, and restored natural ecosystems.

Collectively these collaborations strengthen what I call 'the fabric of health'. This phrase asks us to focus on exploring the threads that build health at every scale—from personal needs woven through communal ones to policies governing our overall environmental health. The questions growing from these collaborations are beginning to show us the need to develop research programs for engaging and accommodating health concerns into the mainstream of our lives.

The Loeb Fellowship Research Initiative is one important venue for facilitating collaborative work of the kind I have been suggesting. Within Harvard's Graduate School of Design, the Loeb Fellowship offers accomplished design practitioners from around the world post-professional awards for independent study. In an effort to extend the intellectual reach of the year-long program, the Fellowship also funds research initiatives for Loeb Fellows from diverse backgrounds to collaborate on important challenges facing the built and natural environment. I am fortunate enough to have participated in three design/health research projects that range from therapeutic design considerations to enhance physical and cognitive rehabilitation to exploring the critical intersection of physical development and public health in challenging urban environments.

The designed environment can be instrumental both in helping individuals cope with ill health and in shaping individual choices that promote health. And this attitude about design can actually transcend any one particular scale. By putting individual human health on a continuum with environmental health, design can help coalesce individual choices into collective ones to make our communities, our cities, and our world more vibrant and equitable.

David Kamp

# FOREWORD

Since the publication of Roger Ulrich's seminal paper in 1984, 'View through a Window may Influence Recovery from Surgery', documenting that hospital patients with a view of trees healed faster and went home sooner than those with a view to a brick wall, the medical world has increasingly recognized the importance of accessible outdoor space. This important study demonstrated that the physical environment had a measurable positive effect on patient health, while it also established a business case for providing access to nature. Many of the improved patient health outcomes, such as duration of hospital stay, and amount of pain medication prescribed, translated directly to potential cost savings. The medical community began to see gardens and accessible outdoor space as not just a cosmetic nicety, but an essential component of the healing environment.

In the past 30 years, more and more gardens have appeared in hospitals, senior care homes, and Alzheimer's facilities. Some of these have been geared to a specific age groups such as the frail elderly or sick children. More recently we have begun to see gardens geared to particular patient needs, such as those with cancer or those recovering from burns. The most successful of these have involved a participatory design process in which the designers have worked collaboratively with the clinical staff, patients, and family members. Another recent trend is the creation of experimental gardens for the treatment of depression or 'burn out syndrome' (in Sweden), and gardens designed for those returning from wars suffering from post traumatic stress disorder (in Denmark, the UK, and the USA).

Parallel with this recognition of the need for gardens in health care, researchers in the fields of environmental psychology, geography, anthropology, and so on have conducted research indicating, for example, the health benefits of street trees, and living close to public green space; the social benefits for low-income residents who have access to green courtyards; and the improved academic performance of high school students whose schools have views to green landscapes. In Japan, a focus has been on the benefits of 'forest bathing'; and in the UK, on the benefits of 'green exercise'. Planners and policy-makers are recognizing that we need to embrace the importance of nature in every kind of environment, not only in health care where people are at their most vulnerable. Thankfully, it appears that humanity is on the cusp of fully understanding what our forbears knew long ago: that we evolved and survived in green landscapes with access to water, and deep in our bodies and our psyches we still need that connection. Now we need it more than ever, now that most of us are living in cities, dependent on our computers, working in air-conditioned offices with little daily contact with nature.

The first contemporary healing gardens appeared in the United States, starting in the mid-1990s. Now the necessity for such beneficial environments in health care as well as in the wider urban environment has been recognized in China, Japan, Australia, Western Europe, and many other parts of the world. In this world context, a book such as this is both welcome and essential. Those of us promoting, researching, or designing restorative outdoor spaces need to learn from each other. It is inspiring to see what is happening in different countries, in different kinds of facilities, and to know that an understanding of the restorative power of nature is now a world-wide phenomenon.

The publication of this book will inform and inspire two groups of readers: the clients and funders of restorative outdoor spaces, and the designers (principally landscape architects) who will translate client needs into beautiful and healing environments.

Clare Cooper Marcus

Professor Emerita, Departments of Architecture and Landscape Architecture University of California, Berkeley

Author (with Naomi Sachs) of *Therapeutic Landscapes: An Evidence-Based Approach to Designing Healing Gardens and Restorative Outdoor Spaces* (Hoboken, NJ: John Wiley and Sons, 2014)

The Notion of Healing Gardens

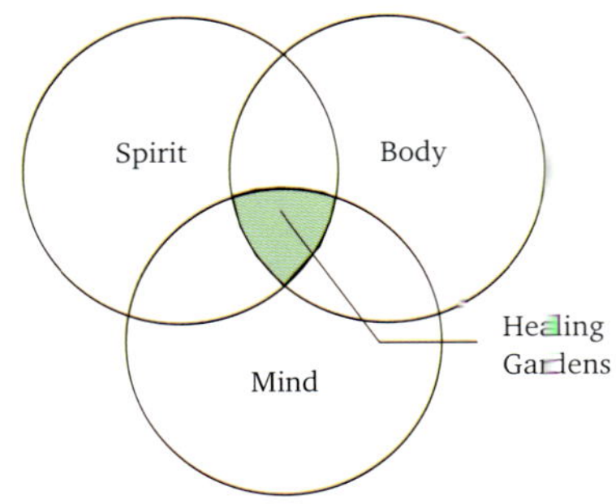


Source: after Vapaa, 2002

# 1/ Healing Garden

Author: Dr. Hesham El Barmelgy
Associate Professor of Urban Design and Sustainable Development Department of Urban Design, Faculty of Regional and Urban Planning, Cairo University
From the paper 'Healing Gardens' Design', published June 2014, International Journal of Education and Research.
(http://www.ijern.com/journal/June-2013/43.pdf)

## 1.1. Introduction

'Health' and 'well-being' have always been indicators for 'quality of life', while 'quality of life' could be perceived as a method of measuring the degree of 'community sustainability'. The World Health Organization (WHO) defines health as 'a state of complete physical, mental and social wellbeing and not merely the absence of disease or infirmity'. 'Health' is this basic need for a connection with nature that keeps people going. A number of studies have been conducted that investigate and prove the connection between nature and healing.

Health studies and horticultural therapeutic programs prove that there is a relationship between health and gardens. Gardens are not only looked at as sources of physical healing but as mental and emotional healing sources as well. The subject of health is always important, as health is something people all strive for and hope to achieve. It is a positive state of life encompassing the entire life situation and environment. The notion of healing gardens should not just be restricted as a requirement for sick people; it is important for healthy people as much as it is important for those who are sick.

## 1.2. The notion of healing gardens

### 1.2.1. Sustainability and the notion of healing gardens

Greenery, as a sustainable form of landscape, has the potential for inducing active living and public health; thus, linking the importance of the natural environment to the built environment and citizens' health. In Western and Eastern communities, it has been noticed that greenery in the city is essential for the health of city dwellers. The brain is capable of two types of attention: directed attention belonging to the higher cognitive centers, and soft fascination linked to the memory part of the brain. In a natural environment, the higher cognitive centers rest while the old part of the brain is stimulated giving the sense of restoration, rest and healing. It is vital for public green areas to be located near residential areas. Studies have proved that natural environments outside a 164-foot (50-meter) radius from residential areas would result in a decrease in the number of visits to the gardens, and an increase in stress levels. These findings emphasize the significance of locating a natural environment directly adjacent to dwellings (Stigsdotter, 2005).

When designing a healing garden it has been noted that 'sight' is the most immediate physical sense that reacts to a garden. Sight is important because a person only needs to open his/her eyes to experience an ever-changing kaleidoscope of light and colour. Research and studies have proven the effect of color on human thoughts, actions, health, and even relationships with others (Vapaa, 2000:64). The human sense of 'smell' is also very important in designing a healing garden. Scientists have discovered that sweet essences produce alpha, theta, and delta brainwave patterns, which lead to a state of total relaxation. Other fragrances could stimulate beta brainwaves inducing a state of alertness in the human brain. If users dislike the produced fragrances of a garden, it would block any effect upon the nervous system that empowered the sense of alertness. It would thus limit the garden's chances of promoting its healing powers. This emphasizes the importance of providing the garden with the proper scents.

If healing gardens are to symbolize health promoters, then they have to offer a considered balance between the body, the mind, and the spirit (Vapaa, 2002). A healing garden is to represent the ability to promote the sustainability status between the three matters as presented in the figure above. Franke (1996) made it clear through his statement that health is the core of the sustainable landscape stating that 'the only path to true sustainability is one which promotes the importance of the health of the local environment' (Franke, 1996:246). Thus, the healing garden can be considered a deep form of sustainable landscape, where both humans and the environment are to mutually benefit from promoting it.

### 1.2.2. History of healing gardens

The idea of healing gardens is both ancient and modern. Following the beginning of human settlements and communities, local healing places were nearly always found in nature (Brown et al., 2010; and Marcus and Barnes, 1999). The earliest hospitals and infirmaries in the Western world were dependent on plants, herbs, and a cloistered garden as essential parts of the healing process. For a long time the importance of health and well-being have been noticed in the presence of urban green space, green ways, parks, green areas, schoolyards, and private gardens. All these factors are viewed as the health-creating elements of the city (Morse et al., 2011; and Stigsdotter, 2005). The great gardens of Egypt were built to offer an escape from the external environment, offering a healing relief. Restorative or healing gardens for the sick have been part of the landscape of healing since medieval times (Clark, 2004).

Gardens were always portrayed as a paradise that offered respite from illness to the healing of the soul and the body. By the end of the 1980s and the start of the 1990s, a decline of the concept was witnessed all around the world. The connection between healing and nature was gradually superseded by advancing treatment technologies and methods. By the late 20th century the idea of nature and healing was totally lost; nature 'landscaping' came to be merely portrayed as a green sort of decoration. Starting from the late 1990s, the idea of healing gardens once again gained interest and began to appear in the research field of sustainable landscape (Vapaa, 2002). Today the notion of healing gardens is gaining popularity due to the harsh living and environmental conditions that people are suffering from all over the world.

### 1.2.3. Defining healing gardens

A garden, in general, is portrayed as a haven where people find a welcoming escape from the everyday stresses of the outside world. On some level all gardens have healing effects (Rawlings, 1998). Vapaa (2002) stated a very important definition explaining functions of a healing garden: he stated that 'instead of stressing the idea that they can cure a person, the benefits are related more to the alleviation of stress and the abilities of the space to soothe, to calm, to rejuvenate, or to restore one's mental and emotional health' (Vapaa, 2002:4). In other words, healing gardens are not just for sick people; they serve both the healthy and the ailing.

A healing garden is able to restore the natural balance in humans so that they do not feel stress and other pressures. It is defined as a category that includes outdoor or indoor garden spaces. Some scholars seem to think that those gardens belong to hospitals and health-care centers (Stigsdotter, 2005), while others see that they are very personal spaces that could be successfully located in private homes. Vapaa (2002) concluded his study stating: 'a healing garden is one where the designer pays close attention to the needs and likes of the user(s) or client(s) and is able to provide therapeutic qualities in the space that addresses them' (Vapaa, 2002:73). Stark (2004) has a vision of the healing garden as a microcosm of the larger world, where each feature of the garden is to represent a larger feature in the landscape. He argues that through this modeling, healing has to be able to 'stimulate the senses, improve immune response, and promote recuperation from physical and emotional illness... a healing garden is a keeper of a sacred place. Its users can access higher levels of spiritual power by their simple presence in its space' (Stark, 2004:3). Stark sees the power of the healing garden in its ability to bring the human back to nature. The nostalgic power of nature, which is embedded in each person's higher cognitive part of the brain, can rest while the old part of the brain is stimulated, thus achieving the healing power. Based on literature analysis, the power of healing gardens lies in its ability to connect humans back into their private imaginative nature. Accordingly, healing gardens is a broad collective term that encompasses various types of gardens that aim to promote health and well-being to humans and the adjacent environment.

### 1.2.4. Types of healing gardens

The positive health effect of staying in urban green spaces has been recognized. If the goal of the community is to promote sustainable development, then in the heart of the sustainability process is the ability to promote better health for all city inhabitants. Studies proved that each dweller has the right to free access to an urban green space within a maximum radius of 164 feet (50 meters) from their residence. Consequently, the types of healing gardens can be classified. The first type of healing gardens is like a sanctuary or a natural reservoir, where nature and wildlife are preserved. This is presented by the city's green infrastructure elements, encompassing the city's open spaces, green ways, nature parks, and green belts. The second type is a meditation garden within the premises of a hospital or a health-care center. Finally, the third type is a privately owned garden. The third type is agreed upon by most healing researchers to be the best type of meditation garden with healing effects. This is based on the fact that the more time a human is in contact with nature, the more profound the healing results will be (Hopper, 2007; Vapaa 2002; and Marcus and Barnes, 1999). A residential or a private garden is the climax of the healing garden typology. It allows the user(s) to gain the maximum benefit from the healing qualities of a garden, because it is their own personal space where they express their individual identity, needs, and level of engagement (Vapaa, 2002).

## 1.3. Healing gardens a facilitator for the users' horticulture and aesthetic needs

A healing garden's main role is to provide a sanctuary to allow for meditation and to fulfill other social and emotional requirements of its user. A talented designer's main job is not only to create a healing garden design but to use their expertise, knowledge, and tools to create a unique garden for the client. As previously discovered from studying the notion, history, and definition of healing gardens along with the users' intervention, one can infer that the designer's ability to integrate the user in the healing garden design process is a key factor for the success of the design. There are various means for achieving such integration between designer and client; the most efficient are personal interviews, written surveys, and questionnaires. During the first session with the client, the designer should investigate some site ideas and gain feedback on them; a good designer should be a good listener. Following the first session, a series of meetings and interviews with the client is a crucial step for determining and fulfilling the clients' social and emotional requirements. The client should be involved in every detail concerning the design. When working on designs for healing premises, the scope of the design capabilities should go far beyond the utilization of the sense of sight to all the other senses. The designer should consider what the client would like to hear, smell, taste, and touch in the garden. The designer should constantly pay attention to the client and if there is any reservation about a certain element of the design, it should be re-considered. It is always easier to re-evaluate and to refine a design than to implement, demolish, and re-implement. Design elements and garden components should be selected carefully and according to the user's needs and opinions. This is done to maximize the healing effects on the environment as well as the user, thus granting the garden a healing label. Client satisfaction is the key issue that determines the success of the design process. The user(s) have to be acknowledged as effective members of the design team. Success in a healing garden is only attained if the garden has managed to relate to its owner at the most personal level.

# 2/ Healthcare Center Outdoor Landscape

Author: Gökçen Firdevs Yücel
Architecture Department, İstanbul Aydın University, İstanbul, Turkey

From the chapter 'Hospital Outdoor Landscape Design' in the book *Advances in Landscape Architecture*, published July 2013.
(http://cdn.intechopen.com/pdfs-wm/45442.pdf)

## 2.1. Introduction

Among public institutions, the large buildings and complicated intervening and surrounding areas of hospitals usually tend to be seen by the public as removed from the urban context, as spaces to be feared, which one only accesses in emergencies or out of necessity. However, this psychological perception of their distance and separation can be decreased by today's more hospitable approaches to their content and design (Marcus and Francis, 1997).

With a growing understanding of the importance of the physical environment for the quality of hospital care and the health and safety of patients and staff, the outdoor spaces of hospitals are beginning to be considered, particularly in scenic and more green areas, as a productive complement to the interior areas, which are reserved for patient treatment and have traditionally been prioritized.

As a result of this new, holistic approach to medicine—which entails alleviating the fears and disorientation of patients that may hinder medical treatment—today's hospital has come to be seen as a necessarily comforting and stress-free environment, created with a broader, patient-oriented sense that encompasses both master planning and landscaping (Fang, 2000).

This means that the outdoor as well as the indoor spaces of hospitals are understood as crucial to patients' physical, psychological, and social recuperation and wellness (Marcus and Francis, 1997; Marcus and Barnes, 1995; Ulrich, 2002; Marcus, 2002; Gupta and Gupta, 2007): appropriately designed active and passive hospital landscapes enhance patients' interaction with nature and so reduce stress, facilitating interaction with others in ways compatible with and complementary to those found in the urban environment (Ulrich, 1984; Ulrich, 2002).

## 2.2. User groups

### 2.2.1. Patients

The health-care environment should be designed taking into account patients' psychological as well as physical needs, disabilities, and duration of stay (Smith, 2007); long-term inpatients or outpatients will have more varied requirements than short-term ones, and their holistic treatment will be enhanced by access to gardens, sheltered outdoor plazas, common social areas, and reading resource areas (American Planning Association, 2012). In addition, patients undergoing different kinds of treatment may use these areas for different purposes: for example, orthopedics patients may need to use walking aids in the gardens; facilities for seniors may need handrails and more shaded areas; physical therapy patients may need to tend to plants at different heights; and psychiatric patients may need 'memory cues' and planted areas, which minimize the risk of injury.

### 2.2.2. Visitors

A supportive environment is also essential for people visiting friends or relatives in the health-care facility, because while visiting patients can be salutary, it may also be emotionally draining (Neducin et al., 2010).

### 2.2.3. Staff

Outdoor spaces are especially important for health-care staff who spend most of their time in the facility, and need designated and accessible areas removed from their daily activities, where they can wander, collect themselves, and adjust to the stress of their work. While administrative staff tend to have the most free time to use outdoor spaces, as they typically have a one-hour lunch and regular breaks (Marcus and Francis, 1997), nurses have to keep patients constantly in view and help them go outdoors. However, nurses generally do not have time to stay with patients outside, and cannot leave them alone, so their responsibilities, as well as the distances from nursing stations to the outdoor spaces, have a negative effect on the use of these spaces by both patients and nurses.

## 2.3. Component and design criteria

### 2.3.1.Hardscape components

#### a. Gateways and entrances

Gateways and entrances welcome people on arrival and provide cues for them to find their way around the site; they can perform this function if a comprehensive network of connecting paths is planned, specified, and followed up to ensure they are properly constructed (Shackell and Walter, 2012). The main entrance should be accessed logically by the most direct path, and the entryway to the outdoor space should have no ramps or steps (Marcus and Francis, 1997). Landscaping, artwork and detailing can prioritize the main access points and create a sense of place, and benches should be available for people arriving or waiting for rides (Main and Hannah, 2010). Entrances must be sufficiently wide to accommodate people with special mobility requirements; for the visually impaired, different kinds of surfacing materials can be helpful, and tactile elements should indicate thresholds (Queensland Health, 1999).

#### b. Parking areas

Parking areas should be sufficient to accommodate staff and employees, and parking should ideally be reserved for staff at the back of the hospital so they do not have to deal with heavy traffic when they come to work (Kunders, 2008). Parking for patients, especially those with disabilities, should be as close as possible to the entrance (Gupta and Gupta, 2007). Patients and visitors unfamiliar with the hospital may easily be confused if parking space is difficult to find; this can be solved by using directional signs that can be altered or moved as conditions change (International Parking Institute, 2009).

#### c. Paths

Large hospital or medical complexes should be organized within a clear circulation hierarchy: main roads, shopping streets, neighborhood streets, and service alleys. Each of these, as well as intersections and destinations, should be indicated by a consistent system of spatial cues (Allison, 2007). This circulation in the health-care facility should be independent of public roadways, and public (non-secured) and private (secured) zones should be distinct, preferably with patient intake and outdoor recreational areas in the private zone. Traffic circulation should be organized so that individuals and ambulances can directly access emergency facilities (American Planning Association, 2012).

The main circulation routes should be clearly indicated, for example, by giving easily understood names to the main corridors, such as 'Hospital Street' or 'Blue Corridor' (here the walls and floor should be predominantly blue in color); or having colored lines along the walls or floor to designate main routes; or using lighting along a route (NHS Estates, 2005). Primary routes should be accessible to everyone; however, some people will prefer to experience the natural environment unmodified and will not expect easy access everywhere (Shackell and Walter, 2012).

Minor walkways should be at least 4 feet 11 inches (1.5 meters) wide, with drainage that will get rid of rainwater quickly. One-way traffic routes should be at least 4 feet 11 inches (1.5 meters) wide to allow for the turning circle of a wheelchair; two-way traffic routes should be at least 6 feet 10 inches (2.1 meters) wide. There is a risk of tripping if the edges of a path are raised (Furgeson, 2012); and handrails or balustrades and wheelchair barriers will prevent people falling where surface levels change, or when entering uneven ground beside paths and paved areas.

In the garden, clear links with different facilities and direct routes are essential. Right-angled corners in paths should be avoided, and slopes designed as follows: a walkway's slope should not exceed 5 percent (i.e. 12 inches/30.48 centimeters of rise for a length of 20 feet/6.1 meters); cross slopes should not exceed 2 percent (12 inches/30.48 centimeters of rise for a length of 50 feet 9 inches/15.24 meters). Where the slope does exceed 1/20 (or 5 percent), there should be a support railing to prevent slipping. The surfaces of paths should be firm, smooth and level, and provide traction; they should reflect the context, with 'softer' materials used for informal settings. Paving surfaces should be smooth enough to be used by wheelchairs and gurneys (Marcus and Barnes, 1995), but grooved paving may be unsuitable for them. Different materials have different advantages and disavantages: concrete is suitable, but costly; asphalt absorbs and radiates heat, and may be too hot in the summer; decomposed granite may be suitable for wheelchairs, but is not for users of crutches. More recently developed rubberized paving materials are firm enough to support wheelchairs, and also absorb the force of a fall.

Outdoor areas should be designed so they can be used throughout the year; snow- or ice-melting devices should be in place for walkways during the winter.

### d. Children's gardens

Children are usually discouraged from moving around in hospital environments lest they disturb the health-care workers or patients; there should be spaces set apart for them where they can move as freely as they need or wish to (Nord, 2009), as they need to engage in imaginative play regardless of the condition of their health. Children need to feel they can create and make changes by interacting with their environment and moving objects and parts; as a result, flexible play areas should be designed to stimulate their imaginations (Verderber and Refuerzo, 2006) and give them the pleasure and therapeutic benefit of creative activity.

A children's area might, in addition to using primary colors and providing climbing structures, include a path maze, a chalkboard masonry wall, child-sized sculptures, or a miniature bridge traversing a faux rock stream, which can also be crossed on stepping stones. Routes should be stable and made of surfaces like decomposed granite, asphalt, wooden boardwalk, resilient mats, and concrete, to resist slipping. There might be platforms so children in wheelchairs can safely move onto and off play structures; and sand play areas may be made available at different heights, so they can be used on the ground or from a wheelchair (Leibrock and Harris, 2011).

### e. Dining areas

Because the dining area is used by more people than any other hospital area, there are more potential outdoor space users in it; having an outdoor space near the dining area is essential (Marcus and Francis, 1997). There should be tables in the space for eating, reading, and writing activities, and to serve as territorial markers, as people rarely intrude on a table that is being used. Umbrella tables with chairs can also be used to provide shade and semi-private group spaces.

### f. Art

Artworks form part of the healing environment, and works of art in health-care facilities featuring images of nature have been linked with stress relief in diverse groups of people. In hospital spaces that can easily be accessed, artworks that create inviting, habitable spaces should be incorporated into the design.

Appropriate artworks can create an engaging focal point for a hospital space. In terms of genre, Ulrich has shown that post-operative patients prefer representational pictures, which tend to incorporate the subdued colors of nature, as opposed to abstract art, which often features unexpected color combinations; another study found that people in a state of anxiety prefer less saturated colors (Shepley, 2006). The artworks should therefore be selected with these effects in mind.

### g. Water

Hearing water running in a fountain, or seeing fish in a pond or sunlight reflecting on water, can be meaningful for a patient (Verderber and Refuerzo, 2006); the sound of running water in particular can mask other noises, which negatively affect the therapeutic value of a space. Such sights and sounds create sensory focal points for garden spaces, which attract all ages and abilities.

Water should be available, close to the garden site, and in a paved area to prevent muddying. The spigot should be 24–36 inches (61–91.5 centimeters) above ground, and hand levers (not round spigot handles) and snap connectors should be used. Soaker hoses and mulch can decrease the water requirements of the garden. 'Bubble' fountains may be appropriate, as they are tactile and make use of shallow water, raising fewer health and safety issues.

### h. Site furniture

This term refers to freestanding elements such as seating, litter bins, lighting, and signs, which should be selected to meet the needs of users. Furniture should be anchored to concrete pads or too heavy to be moved, and in cases where there is a risk of users running away, it should not be placed near fences or walls (Epstein, 2006)

## 2.3.2. Softscape components

### a. Landscaped grounds

Green areas between buildings, primarily used for waiting and eating in, link the architecture with walking paths; however, they may be expensive to maintain.

- **Seating**

Seating should be available where people would actually want to use it, typically enclosed and toward the back, facing an attractive view or focal point, and not obstructing people on the path. Comfortable, movable, and varied seating can increase usage of the garden, especially by hospital staff; there should be benches and chairs for individuals, and more social seating arrangements for groups (Main and Hannah, 2010). Social seating arrangements (right-angled or centripetal benches, or movable chairs) should be conveniently located near the garden entrance, where they are most likely to be used by staff for short breaks (Marcus and Barnes, 1995). In addition to semi-private areas, there should be some benches arranged in a line rather than in a group, facing a view or circulation area.

Benches are usually situated at rest places or corridors with an exterior view (Verderber and Refuerzo, 2006). Space should be left beside a seat to accommodate a wheelchair or electric scooter. Raised features can help wheelchair users and people who cannot easily bend down, and should attract others as well—for example, if the edge can serve as an informal seat. The thinnest construction materials should be used, as long as they are stable, to increase the area of the garden: seating ledges should be 8 inches to 1 foot 5½ inches (20–45 centimeters) wide, and the sides may range from 1 foot 5½ inches (45 centimeters) high for a child, to 1 foot 11½ inches (60 centimeters) for a visitor sitting by a bed, to 2 feet 5½ inches (75 centimeters) or more for those who cannot bend easily.

Seats can be artworks in themselves. The material used should not retain heat or cold, so concrete, aluminum and steel should not be used: wood or hard plastic are preferable. Moveable chairs can be rearranged depending on the sun or shade, and to adjust the size of the seated group. In general, seats should have arm and back support, but their height and depth, as well as their supporting structure, will affect their usefulness to people with special needs, and this should be taken into consideration (Shackell and Walter, 2012).

- **Signage**

Being able to choose whether or not to follow or avoid a route that might have rough paths is essential; appropriate, approachable, and welcoming signs are a must. Site signage should indicate, among other things, directional or one-way traffic, restrictions, parking, deliveries, patient entry points, entrances to facilities, and so on (Epstein, 2006). Tactile signs should be fixed at a height of 4 feet 11 inches (150 centimeters) or 3 feet 11 inches (120 centimeters) for children (Leibrock and Harris, 2011). Other sensory indicators, such as audible water features and wind chimes, may also be used to assist wayfinding for the visually impaired in the garden.

- **Lighting**

The primary purpose of lighting is to enhance safety and security. Exterior lighting deters thieves; lights on stairs, walkways or approach roads both increase safety from attackers and help prevent accidental falls. Parking areas, entrance and service roads, and also isolated or dark areas need to be clearly defined and lit; bollards or bulkheads are usually used for this purpose. Lighting along pedestrian routes should be mounted at a height where faces can be seen and recognized. Any entrances, intersections or hazards, such as changes in path level, should be indicated by beacons. An added therapeutic benefit of nighttime lighting is that it enables safe use of the space at night, and viewing of the garden from indoors (Marcus and Barnes, 1995).

- **Receptacles**

The locations of trash containers should be considered an essential element of health-care facility planning, as they allow for easy disposal of food and paper products outdoors. The number of receptacles required depends on the population density and the activity level in an area, as well as how often they are emptied; overflowing litter bins indicate a need either for more of them or for more frequent service. There should be litter containers at all transition areas, such as doors, building entries, parking access points, and social and pedestrian spaces. To provide a less disturbing environment, receptacles should be placed at least 11 feet 10 inches (3.6 meters) away from where people tend to socialize (Main and Hannah, 2010).

### b. Landscaped setbacks

These are usually planted areas in front of the main entrance, which are visually pleasant and serve to separate the health-care center building from the street.

### c. Front porches

These may include overhangs or porch roofs, an area where vehicles can pick up or drop off passengers, sitting areas, signs with directions, a mailbox, telephone booth, bus stop, and so on.

### d. Entry gardens

These are visually pleasant green spaces designed like gardens and located near health-care-center entrances.

### e. Courtyards

Courtyards are the central and most often used spaces in a hospital building complex, because of their proximity to the dining area; they tend to be used more by visitors and patients if they are easily visible, and should be sufficiently large to prevent overcrowding (Marcus and Francis, 1997). Courtyard features may include landscaped tree-shaded areas, water features, flower beds, and moveable seats; for reasons of privacy and security as well as aesthetics, they may be fenced (especially if designed for care of the mentally ill) up to a height of 14 feet (4.27 meters) (Department of Veterans Affairs, 2010).

### f. Plazas

These outdoor areas, which are typically paved and furnished, should allow easy access to wheelchairs, walkers, and crutches. They should include shade from flowering trees or spreading evergreens, and at least a quarter of the trees should be above the minimum specified size. A plaza should have shaded seating areas decorated with plants, colored shrubs and ground cover, and perhaps a water feature. Because these areas are largely paved, landscaping and gardening maintenance costs are low.

## g. Roof terraces

A roof terrace is usually a long, narrow balcony occupying one side of the roof of a hospital building. The elements it is composed of (plants and seating) and the surface finish are designed to minimize observation from higher buildings overlooking it. Roof terraces are sometimes too exposed to wind, heat or shade, and for this reason care must be taken when selecting their location (Marcus and Barnes, 1995).

## h. Roof gardens

Gardens located on roofs are visually attractive, enabling patients to look out from their rooms and have a comforting view of grass, paving stones, benches, and people, rather than roofing material or medical equipment. Depending on how much planting material is used and to what depth, green roofs generally weigh between 15 pounds (6.82 kilograms) and 50 pounds (22.7 kilograms) per square foot. They are a practical and sustainable way of regulating the quantity and speed of runoff, as they retain 70–90 percent of the rainwater that falls on them in summer, and 35–40 percent of the precipitation in winter (Schucker, 2010). Roof gardens enable major energy savings that will more than compensate, in time, for the costs of building, waterproofing, and landscape maintenance; and they also minimize the environmental impact of a health-care facility.

## i. Healing gardens

Gardens, which serve as safe and meditative environments for healing and recuperation, date back to the medieval period, and have traditionally been features of hospitals, hospices, rehabilitation centers, and nursing homes (Gerlach-Spriggs et al., 2004). The wide range of activities related to healing gardens may be passive or active: looking at the garden from a window, sitting, eating, reading, doing paperwork or taking a nap in the garden, prayer and meditation, walking to a preferred spot, gardening, exercise and sports, and children's play. The gardens are conducive to stress relief, relieving physical symptoms, and enhancing the feeling of well-being of hospital staff and patients.

Successful healing gardens make use of certain fundamental design principles:

*Enhance feelings of control*: People should be aware that there is a garden and be able to find, enter, and use its space. The garden should have private areas that cannot be seen from overlooking windows, and different kinds of spaces so users can feel they are making choices; if users are also consulted in designing the garden, this will also add to their feeling of control. All or some of the five senses can be chosen as focal stimuli in the garden's construction (Vapaa, 2002).

*Have a prevalence of green material and areas*: Patients' sense of well-being is enhanced by soft landscapes, so plant material should be dominant and hardscaping reduced to a minimum: trees, shrubs, and flowers should make up about 70 percent of the garden, with 30 percent in walkways and plazas (Franklin, 2012).

*Encourage exercise*: Designs should provide easy access and independence, as well as stress-reducing structural elements, such as walking paths for patients to encourage exercise, and play areas for children (Severtsen, 2006).

*Provide positive distractions*: Stress levels among patients have been shown to decrease when they are in the presence of plants, flowers, and water features as well as when they are engaged in gardening. In the Child and Adolescent Mental Health Unit at Great Ormond Street Hospital, growing vegetables has been seen to have therapeutic value for young people with eating disorders; and flower and cutting gardens are being utilized for horticultural therapy at London's Bow Centre (Shackell and Walter, 2012).

*Minimize intrusions*: Gardens should be designed to minimize negative factors like urban noise, smoke, and artificial lighting, in favor of natural lighting and sounds. Gardens that appeal to the different senses are ideal (although strongly scented flowers and other scents should be avoided for chemotherapy patients) (Franklin, 2012).

*Minimize ambiguity*: Complex or mysterious settings that provide a challenge might be of interest to the healthy, but research shows that abstract design may be contraindicated for patients who are ill or undergoing stress. For this reason, the use of abstract art may be unsuitable, and design should focus on clearly identifiable elements.

## j. Meditation gardens

This type of small, enclosed, quiet garden is designed with a central focal point to help patients (often a single patient at any given time, depending on the size) concentrate and relax as part of the healing process. It is a space for quiet contemplation, removed from distractions and private—that is, not visible from other indoor spaces. Meditation gardens are labeled as such and purpose-designed, and their layout is usually simple and minimalist, comprising, for example, a circle representing life, a square symbolizing order, or symbols such as the Celtic knot, which represents travel (Marcus and Barnes, 1995). They usually have a lawn and/or a comfortable seating area with a focal point, typically a water feature, to encourage meditation. The vegetation should provide cool colors, such as violets, blues and greens, rather than bright, warm or contrasting colors (Furgeson, 2012).

### k. Viewing gardens

Some health-care facilities with limited space and budgets feature small, enclosed gardens that can be seen but not entered. Such gardens cost little to maintain; provide some green space, flowers, and perhaps a water feature; and they can be seen from sheltered indoor seating areas. However, the elements of nature they provide are removed from the senses, as they cannot be approached smelled, heard, or touched.

### l. The viewing/walk-in garden

In this variation on a viewing garden, the green space can actually be entered from a corridor or waiting room. Because it has limited space and seating, it remains a quiet area that does not disturb the privacy of any nearby rooms or offices, and also provides a comforting view for people waiting or passing by in the corridor. The main disadvantage is that people using the space may feel a lack of privacy, as they can be watched by others (Marcus and Barnes, 1995).

### m. Edible gardens

A healing garden can be developed to a new dimension if herbs, fruit plants, and vegetables are grown together with the usual planted vegetation in an easily accessible space. This 'edible garden' should be simple and balanced, but designed in a repeating pattern with wandering paths demarcating public and private spaces (Parcell, 2012). The vegetation would favor annuals over perennials, and the garden could feature a large number and variety of plants. A good example is the Nasturtium species, which has beautiful flowers that can also be eaten.

## 2.3.3. Guideline

When creating a garden for a health-care facility, the focus should be on location, accessibility, patients' requirements and preferences, and the design elements to be included (Epstein, 2006). The garden should have opportunities for mobility and exercise, present a choice between social and solitary spaces, and facilitate beneficial distraction and direct or indirect interaction with nature.

### a. Accessibility

This is an essential requirement, both within the hospital and in its environment. Gardens may be designed and set up attractively, but people need to be aware that they exist, that they are easily accessible through entrances and paths, that they are useable regardless of people's age or disability, and that they facilitate certain activities. Within the garden, visitors follow internal circulation routes, typically between walls, but occasionally crossing open spaces. Paths help people to find their way in hospitals, and differentiating them can help patients and visitors find their way (Allison, 2007).

### b. Visibility

The more a garden is visible and people are aware of it, the more its activity areas and paths will be preferred. At least one outdoor space should be visible or its location clearly indicated from the main entrance (Piotrowsk, 2007). Patients' rooms should have views of the garden so they can enjoy it even if they are unable to visit it (Sadler, 2007).

### c. Feeling of control

Research shows that a feeling of lack of control can lead to or aggravate depression, passivity, elevated blood pressure, and decreased immune-system operation. Getting users involved in its design can enhance a sense of control in the garden. Different types of spaces and layouts can enable them to make their own choices—for example, a variety of pathways, of types of nooks where they can sit, of furniture (if some is moveable), or of views, ranging from close to distant (Marcus, 2010).

### d. Feeling of security

Patients often feel both physically and psychologically vulnerable in hospitals, and a feeling of security should be provided. This includes sufficient lighting and public telephones in isolated areas so people can call for help, and other facilities and design elements in the garden that make them feel safe. Broadly speaking, there should be a feeling of enclosure but without the feeling that one is being watched. Features should include handrails and seating at frequent intervals, particularly near the entrance to assist the elderly, the disabled and mobility-impaired, and avoid paving materials like asphalt that reflect a strong glare (Marcus, 2002).

### e. Physiological comfort

As hospital patients are often sensitive to temperature (burn patients, for example generally have to keep out of direct sunlight), options such as sunny and shady areas should be provided, as well as seating shielded from breezes by plants or structures. Various medications require patients to avoid sunlight; some patients might be afraid of catching a chill if they go outdoors. Other patients have trouble getting up on their feet, so the garden should have garden seats with arms and backs, and also benches one can sprawl or lie on.

### f. Quiet

Research on four hospital gardens showed that users were

disturbed by sounds of machines like air-conditioners and traffic noise; areas to be used as garden spaces should be planned in advance, away from traffic, parking areas, delivery driveways, and helicopter landing pads. A garden designed for therapeutic purposes should be quiet and removed from sounds inside the hospital, which range from public announcements, to television sets to catering trolleys and gurneys; visitors to the garden should feel calm, and be able to hear reassuring sounds such as birdsong, wind chimes, or flowing water.

### g. Familiarity

Hospitals may cause stress for patients and their families, as they are unfamiliar environments, and they can be made more comforting and familiar if they include aspects of nature (Kaplan and Kaplan, 1983). People working in hospitals similarly experience stress, and need to have access to familiar and relaxing garden settings. The aesthetic of the health-care environment should therefore be based on this fundamental need and provide spaces on a human or domestic scale as well as familiar-looking plants and furniture; this is particularly important in facilities for Alzheimer's patients and the terminally ill.

### h. Flexibility

Exterior spaces should attract people, invite them in and engage them; they should be designed based on when (at what times and in what weather conditions), by whom (what groups), and how they are currently used (for example, for a lunch break, exercise, or socializing), and also on how their usage may be shaped in the future. To maintain interest and year-round interaction, for instance, they should be studied to see how they are used in different seasons, and then designed with different seasonal blooms and colors and different weather conditions taken into account.

### i. Sustainability

Resources should be allocated intelligently when designing outdoor spaces: every material used does not have to be green, and some hard surfaces like concrete can help prevent storm water run-off. Wild grasses and Sedum species create groundcover, which reduces domestic grass, decreasing the cost of maintaining lawns. Xeriscaping (designing with low-water-use plants), together with native vegetation, also helps reduce water use and maintenance. Nature trails enable users to have exercise, education, and a natural aesthetic at a minimal cost; and solar-powered lights and water features that recycle rainwater can also be cost-effective and sustainable.

## 2.4. Planting design

As noted earlier, plants that require little water beyond the establishment period and can tolerate the urban environment and climate changes should take precedence in hospital garden planning. Other types of vegetation with varied densities should be used to connect greenways and wildlife corridors and native vegetation should be mixed with compatible new plants in such a way as to sustain both. Native trees are particularly useful as they attract local wildlife. Plant species that attract butterflies bring an atmosphere of gentleness; while additional features (fountains or birdbaths, a bird feeder, trees appropriate for roosting or nesting) may be used to attract birds, which stimulate the senses with their colors and sounds and raise people's morale.

A dark woodland environment might feel oppressive, so open, sunny glades and generous paths are preferable for the health-care environment: they help wild flowers to grow, and enhance the sensory aspects of nature (Shackell and Walter 2012). Seasonally changing flowering trees, shrubs and perennials bring a comforting awareness of life's rhythms and cycles; and using vegetation that provides contrast and harmony through textures, forms, colors and arrangements draws people's attention and focus away from themselves.

Large canopy trees create shade in summer and provide shelter in winter; they can help modify the local climate and reduce the air temperature. Trees with foliage that moves in the breeze attract the gaze to patterns of colors, shadows, light, and movement, providing a soothing and meditative experience (Marcus and Barnes, 1995). In mental-health facilities with high security, trees can soften and screen off the sight of security fences, and can also be planted in areas that patients can access under supervision. Shrubs should be trimmed to emphasize their natural form, so the space looks well cared for and sends the implied message that patients are also well cared for.

For all users of the garden, including the partially sighted, scented and brightly coloured flowers and leaves provide an attractive sensory experience. The olfactory sense is closely associated with memories and feelings, so scents can suddenly stimulate memories and responses, aiding those with memory loss. Sensory stimulation is particularly important for the visually impaired and for patients with reduced cognitive function, and this can be assisted by plants that are colorful throughout the year, are scented (such as Lavandulaspecies and Echinacea species), and have tactile qualities (such as Festucacaesia). Fruit trees can be good for smaller spaces, and offer seasonal attractions.

The edible garden is a useful concept, particularly if the produce can be used in the facility's kitchens. Long-term residents will be able to experience the seasonal development of the garden, and patients in day centers will be able to participate in tending the garden at any time of the year. An activities program might focus on food-growing—for example, eating fruit crumble, or painting berries (Shackell and Walter, 2012). Planting an orchard also puts a site that is only available for a short time to good use.

Precautions should be taken when planting to ensure that there are no hazardous or thorny plants, especially in gardens for children or psychiatric patients, and also no plants that drop slippery fruit or leaves that might constitute a hazard (Queensland Health, 1999). Low shrubs and dense, dark vegetated 'walls' that obscure the view should not be planted near sidewalks; instead, these areas should be planted with year-round screens whose appearance is softened by varied deciduous plants and open spaces.

Elevated gardens can be designed for the use of patients in wheelchairs; here pots and planters should be raised to a height of at least 24 inches (61 centimeters) and should be accessible from all sides if they exceed this depth. This kind of vertical garden can be used easily by both ambulatory and seated patients.

Raised planter boxes can be set up in some areas and looked after by patients in wheelchairs or on motorized scooters; this adds area to the garden at minimal cost. The width of the plant beds should be at most 4 feet 11 inches (1.5 meters) if they can be accessed from all sides, or 2 feet 5½ inches (75 centimeters) if they are used from one side. More area can also be added to the raised bed through the use of structural extensions.

Table planters are shallow, soil-filled trays supported on legs. These raised planters, which are the same width as raised planters, need a height of about 2 feet 3½ inches (70 centimeters) of free space below them (including knee clearance) to allow people to sit on chairs and tend them. The soil containers should be 8–9½ inches (20–25 centimeters) deep, so the total height of the structure is about 2 feet 10 inches–3 feet (87.5–92.5 centimeters), with the top of the planter no higher than the rib cage of the seated person (Leibrock and Harris, 2011).

The site should be well maintained, for therapeutic as well as physical safety reasons. In comparison with patio structures and spaces, shrubs, trees, and flowers are more difficult to maintain, but they provide the most therapeutic benefits. Suitable fertilizing, selective thinning rather than shearing, and the use of seasonal color are important factors conducive to the characteristics of the garden that users prefer (Marcus and Barnes, 1995); hand weeding, mulching, companion planting, and the proper spacing of plants will decrease the use of chemical fertilizers. In short, a poorly maintained environment offends their dignity and has a negative effect on the morale of patients.

# 3/ Children's Therapeutic Garden

Author: Ismail Said
Associate Professor, PhD
School of Graduate Studies, University Teknologi Malaysia
From *Design Considerations and Recommendations for the Development of Children Therapeutic Garden in Malaysian Hospital*, published 2008.

## 3.1. Introduction

The planning and designing of outdoor spaces in assisting the healing process of children in the hospital environment is new but full of potential in the health-service sector in Malaysia. Experiencing the natural environment would nurture ill children through the provision of a space to play and discover. Through passive and/or active interaction with the garden elements, the children are able to get away from the confinement of ward conditions and the routines of medical treatments. With proper design and implementation, the hospital outdoor spaces can be made into therapeutic platforms for the children to play, rest, and socialize.

The design must turn the space into a structured place of respite for the children's bodies and minds. Here they can experience diversity of forms, colors, shapes of landscape elements, and dynamism of climatic factors—namely light, wind, and rain. All their senses can be stimulated by the garden environment, leading to a sense of discovery and a reduction in stress. Stress reduction is a crucial step in the recuperation process. This would result in several positive physiological outcomes including lower blood pressure, reduced muscle tension, and lower skin conductance. Furthermore, patients experiencing a reduction of stress would also display some psychological responses. In children, the responses are known as psychological peacefulness, and adjustments include less crying, more cooperation, and more acceptance of the clinical treatments given by caregivers at the hospitals.

## 3.2. Design considerations and recommendations

### 3.2.1. Site planning and zoning

**a.** Site the garden on a level terrain. Any change of level in the garden will cause difficulty of access.

**b.** Conserve natural features of the site. Natural features—such as mature trees, rock outcroppings, and watercourses—should be conserved as they provide natural identity to the site and potentially useful amenities. A large, canopied tree provides shade for a play space. Play equipment—such as a tree house or a slide on a sand base—is appropriate to be installed for active play.

▸ Conserving a shade tree provides a play space for the children underneath it.

**c.** Locate the garden so patients can view it from their beds. Hence, caregivers can draw the curtains or louvers for them to view the outdoors.

▸ The garden should be located beside the pediatric ward for easy visual and physical access.

**d.** Whenever possible, locate the garden beside the playroom to link both play spaces for the children. In addition, incorporate any transition space such as a patio or wide corridor with the garden. This will add to the diversity of playing or resting zones for the patients and their caregivers.

### 3.2.2. Security

Locate the garden so that it is enclosed on all sides and inaccessible from the public surroundings of the hospital facility except through the security-controlled entrance of the hospital. Patients and caregivers must be protected from intrusive, unwanted social interactions. The enclosure can be in the form of hedges, a fence with climbers, a mural or textured walls of surrounding buildings. They should be strong enoughto stop people from entering the garden as well as pleasant to be viewed by the patients and caregivers. Furthermore, bright and fragrant flowers and murals would become interactive features for the children to use as tools for play. Nectar-laden flowers (such as Thundbergia, Ixoras, Cuphea, and Osbekia) would attract insects such as honeybees, bumblebees and butterflies, and thus add to the diversity of natural features in the garden.

◂ Walls and fences are important to ensure the security of the children while playing in the garden.

### 3.2.3. Microclimate

**a.** Provide a sufficient number of shelters from the afternoon sun and rain. A garden pavilion and dense-to-moderate canopy trees are appropriate to shelter patients and caregivers from the intense sunlight that occurs between 10:30 am and 5:00 pm. The intensity of light adds to the warm equatorial temperature reaching 33°C around 2:00 pm. The pavilion is the resting space for caregivers to supervise the children playing in the garden. The patients should not be allowed to be in the garden in heavy rain as it may cause a detrimental effect on them. Hence, the use of the patio or covered corridor for outdoor play should be maximized during rainy and hot afternoons.

◂ Pavilion provides a shelter for the children from sun and rain.

**b.** Locate the tree at an appropriate distance that would not cast deep shade to the ward, possibly 16½–19½ feet (5–6 meters) from the building, to allow sunlight to be diffused into the building.

**c.** Sunlight provides motion, variety, information, and orientation. By allowing the children into the garden, they will be able to experience the natural light that will stimulate their senses to understand the passage of time, to estimate the time of day, and to enjoy the plant varieties and garden accessories.

▲ Shades from buildings and trees, and the effect of wind would create thermal comfort for gardens' users.

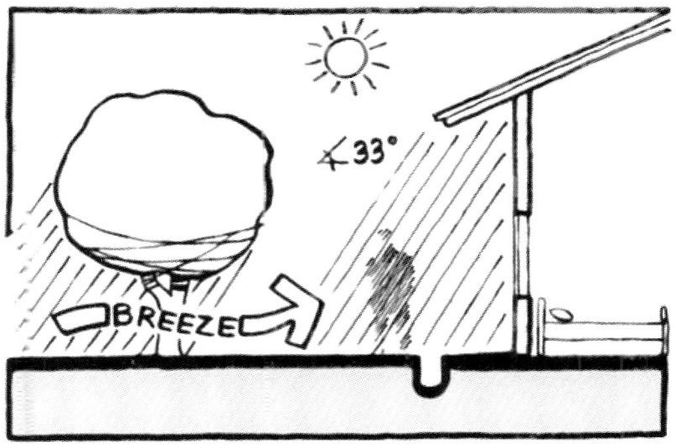


d. Provide one or two timber seats under the shade trees for caregivers to rest.

e. Make the children notice the pattern of shadows and use of light that provide opportunities for motion, variety, orientation, and discovery.

### 3.2.4. Accessibility and circulation

a. Provide accessibility to children of all abilities, including the ones using wheelchairs and walkers. Accessibility obviously plays a big role in effective functioning, both in getting to and from the space, as well as in facilitating movements within the space. An environment that fosters effective functioning also often provides a sense of safety and competence: people like to feel comfortable within a space. Thus, the garden spaces should be linked by a continuous route system without any level change. All open drains along building aprons should be covered with UPVC grating to facilitate accident-free crossing.

b. Provide a clear hierarchy of pathways. Primary paths should provide a relatively direct route to the garden. Place a portal on the primary path to indicate the entrance into the garden.

▶ A clear hierarchy of pathways will ease wayfinding for the children and their caregivers

c. Provide even, tactile surfaces on all paths. The texture of paved materials should vary to stimulate the tactile sense when children walk on them barefoot.

d. In a small garden—where the size ranges from 3229–7535 square feet (300–700 square meters) as can be found in nucleus hospitals—definite pathways are not necessary. Let the children walk freely on lawn that acts as a base for all play zones. This planning method allows the children to make their own selection of play space and equipment, and permits them to make their own decisions. Hence, they will feel fascinated by being in the garden.

### 3.2.5. Planting and composition

a. Compose a coherent and a balanced planting scheme in the garden consisting of flowering and foliage plants, fruiting and shading plants. A coherent character helps to provide a sense of order in the garden and to direct attention. Repetitive planting of shrubs and groundcovers may attain this character. A fruit tree can be set in a mass of foliage shrubs; the tree becomes the main feature, as accent element surrounded by shrubs as a base or backdrop.

b. When space is available, create a hidden setting using a mass planting. A seating space with timber seat over lawn is secluded by compact planting of low and tall shrubs, creating a mysterious setting that invites intrigue and exploration.

◤ Coherent and balanced planting composition provides a sense of order and variety for the garden.

c. Plants and flowers should depict the variety of color, texture, fragrance, and fruits. Fragrances often trigger memories of particular times, events, places, or feelings.

d. Set a large lawn area that will become the base for other planting compositions to be laid in the garden. It is recommended that the minimum length of lawn is about 32 feet 9 inches (10 meters), allowing the children to run or to chase their peers, and even to roll. The lawn should become the central space for spatial organization of resting and play spaces in the garden. It is a favorite space for children to run and walk.

◢ Lawn is a base for the children to perform various activities.

◢ A clay urn could become an interesting storage for toys in the garden setting.

**e.** Introduce plants that attract wildlife, especially insects and birds. Thus, nectar-producing flowers and small-to-medium-sized fruit trees are appropriate for the purpose.

**f.** Conserve existing mature trees that later on can be used as a play structure.

**g.** Introduce fruit trees that are commonly found in house gardens to create a homelike environment.

◀ Introducing common plants such as banana trees creates a home-like environment for the children to familiarise the garden setting.

**h.** Provide planting boxes or beds for sowing seeds and tending the seedlings. Growing plants is an interactive relationship that results in improvement of self-esteem and confidence. Gardening is active play for children, which helps in rehabilitating their gross-motor movement.

### 3.2.6. Garden structures and accessories

**a.** Provide different forms of play equipment and garden structures that will generate a variety of modes of play. Similar to planting composition, forms and colors of the features will directly stimulate the children's senses. For example, a large but low, natural-colored clay urn is appropriate as a treasure chest for storing toys in the garden. Its color will be in contrast to the surrounding planting mass, allowing children to recognize the urn as storage for toys.

**b.** Provide a sufficient number of pavilions and seats for parents and hospital staff to supervise the children while experiencing the garden.

**c.** Provide an opportunity for children to touch and feel with water. A simple feature such as a low urn with fish and water plants would create curiosity in children.

**d.** Draw a cartoon-like mural on the ward's wall to enliven the ambiance of the garden. Leave some portions of the drawings for the patients to complete by coloring with emulsion (water-soluble) paints. By completing a drawing and gaining praise from their caregivers, the patients' self-esteem will increase.

**e.** Allow the children to bring their own toys into the garden. If they insist on bringing home the toys that are stored in the treasure chest of the garden, permit them to take them home. This action would make them feel the garden is part of them.

# 4/ Outdoor Spaces for Elder Populations

Author: David Kamp, FASLA, LF
Founding Principal, Dirtworks, PC Landscape Architecture

From 'Design Considerations in the Design of Outdoor Spaces for Elder Populations', published March 2011 on the University of Virginia School of Architecture Center for Design and Health website. (http://uvadesignhealth.org/resources/)

## 4.1 Introduction

Time spent in a garden plays a critical role in the maintenance and restoration of health. This is true for the young and old, for the healthy as well as the frail. Successfully incorporating nature in Senior Living and Elder Care settings is predicated on enhanced communication. The greatest need at this time is to understand the value of a collaborative approach to design—one that incorporates a working team of designers, health-care professionals, and other advocates. Communication and a close collaborative working relationship are paramount in creating an effective and responsive design.

### 4.1.1 Understanding the site

Understanding and assessing the proposed garden site is an essential first step in order to effectively plan and integrate the design's program and objectives with the site's particular opportunities and constraints. Consider the following:

**• Site history**
Consider the site's previous uses for interesting natural, historical, or cultural features to be incorporated, or negative associations to be addressed (such as abandoned underground structures and soil contamination).

**• Climate**
Local climate, prevailing breezes, and the site's microclimate will influence plant selection, growth, and the garden's use. Surrounding buildings can modify the garden's microclimate, providing shelter and protection from sun and wind, and often extend opportunities for the garden's use.

**• Site surrounds**
Should the site harmonize or provide a distinctive setting to its surroundings? Without a surrounding landscape for consideration, such as a courtyard setting, consider how to create a 'space away' within a confined setting. Regardless of the setting, consider the proposed garden's access, security and privacy for the surrounding resident windows

**• Orientation**
A garden's orientation influences the use of outdoor facilities. Location and orientation should consider uses at different times of day and different seasons. North–south orientations provide benefits during different seasons while east–west orientations provide benefits during different times of day.

**• Site topography**
Gradients have a physical and economic effect on-site development. Their modification may be a constraint or an opportunity, such as creating easily accessible raised beds. Flat sites might incorporate subtle grade changes for interest and a sense of enclosure.

**• Views**
Select and enhance a variety of active and passive views for varying interests and to highlight seasonal changes in evergreen and deciduous plant materials. For courtyard gardens, consider the views across the exterior space to and from resident rooms, activity rooms, and so on.

**• Existing site features**
Existing features can provide opportunities and constraints. Existing trees can provide immediate and essential shade along with seasonal interest, but they also require careful protection during construction. In weighing the merits of existing trees, consider their proximity to construction and site disturbance, their age and health, along with their species, as some are more resilient to disturbance than others.

**• Soil conditions**
Soil and subsurface conditions are important as the growing medium for plants, providing a suitable base for pavements and foundations, and to provide proper drainage. Poorly draining soils may require remedial treatment to achieve proper drainage and may be particularly susceptible to compaction during building construction.

**• Site pollutants**
Consider the effects of on-site and off-site conditions and activities, including fumes and noise. Whenever possible, locate mechanical equipment outside of and away from the garden. Consider the effects of mechanical exhausts and prevailing winds on the garden ambiance.

**• Utility services**
Existing and proposed utilities require coordination to avoid conflicts with planting, garden uses, views, foundations, access, and maintenance. Carefully coordinate utility service layouts, along with water and power service for the garden early in the design process.

**• Access and phasing**
Consider long-term access needs for maintenance and security and the immediate needs for construction. The width and placement of access doors should be coordinated with anticipated maintenance needs.Consider advancing portions of the planting for expediency and cost-efficiency.

## 4.1.2. Understanding the users

The goals of the garden are the goals of the staff. The project team should collectively explore opportunities for the garden to engage residents, offer a range of activities, and help to achieve specific therapeutic outcomes. To better understand the opportunities the garden offers, consider the following questions as starting points in the team discussion:

- How can the garden address varying physical considerations and achieve individual goals, such as providing exercise and improved manual dexterity?
- How can the garden support psychological considerations, such as independence and socialization?
- How might the garden engage residents in helpful daily tasks that engender a sense of contribution and belonging (such as checking bird feeders, tending plants, and raising the flag)? And how might those 'helpful tasks' benefit other goals, such as exercise, dexterity, and motor-coordination skills?
- What programs are currently underway or planned?
- Should there be structured, casual, and spontaneous activities? What are the daily routines and how are special events handled? Who participates? How can families, friends, and visiting children enjoy the garden? Is there a garden, or a separate area, for staff too?

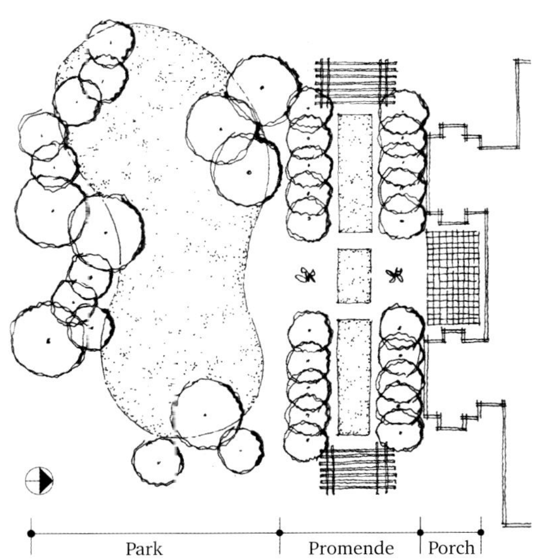


◀ Garden concept plan

The Concept Plan establishes the basic structure to the open space, including important relationships, adjacencies, and scale. In this plan, a progression of spaces is desired: a protected porch; a structured area for activities; and an open park-like setting.

### 4.1.3. Understanding the concerns

Many elderly people face physical challenges inherent in the aging process. Hence, it is important to determine if the people who will be using the garden will require motorized vehicles, walkers, or wheelchairs. For example, will there be people with severe vision impairment, those who cannot bend easily because of the aging process, and others who will need a resting place? These varying, incremental and progressive physical limitations must be considered when determining specific programs and design elements. Consider the following:

**• The aging process**
Of particular concern are the physical challenges inherent in the aging process. A range of abilities needs to be accommodated, including individuals requiring wheelchairs and walkers; those who stoop or cannot bend easily; those requiring frequent rests; and those that may need assistance with activities. These concerns influence the pathway design; the placement of chairs and benches; features and activity areas; and the design of architectural components, such as the width of a porch. For example, benches and chairs should be plentiful but carefully placed to encourage walking in the garden and to provide a choice of settings and destinations. Structured shade near the entry (porches, trellises, and so on) provide a progression of light levels and protective spaces when entering the garden—an important consideration for individuals to comfortably adjust to changing light levels and exposure to the elements.

**• Perception**
The garden must not only be safe, it must be perceived to be safe. The entire garden should be clearly visible from key interior and exterior places. For example, a porch with clear views of the garden allows staff to keep an eye on individual residents while leading a group activity on the porch. A greenhouse window in a kitchen or activity room provides a prominent display area for seasonal activities while also providing staff with a clear view of the garden. To ensure a sense of security and comfort, pathways should be firm and level with clear circulation, destinations, and frequent places to pause and rest.

**• Physical limitations**
Injuries from falls are a major concern, as are diminished strength, stamina, and visual acuity, varying sensory abilities, sunlight sensitivity, awareness, and sense of orientation. Elderly adults with gait problems, Parkinson's disease, severe arthritis and those recovering from strokes are vulnerable to falls. Falls occur at times other than when people are walking. In a garden, people may fall getting in and out of wheelchairs, on and off benches and chairs, or near doors as they try to open them. Diminished sight adds to the problem. Sunlight levels are a concern as certain medications cause sun sensitivity while others may interfere with an individual's ability to regulate body temperature.

**• Health and safety**
Regulatory issues regarding health and safety vary with resident groups and care settings. These are routinely discussed with architects, but rarely between landscape architects and health-care professionals. While interior courtyards and atriums are regulated as interior spaces, regulatory issues with regard to exterior gardens are almost non-existent. In addressing exterior conditions, discussions typically focus on concerns related to injuries, plant toxins, and allergies. The discussions are invaluable in helping clients make informed decisions regarding the design of both the interior and exterior garden spaces.

**• Poisonous plants and insects**
Adults with dementia and visiting children need protection from toxic plants. In addition to common allergies to poison ivy, poison oak, and sumac, many plants (even common bulbs) can be irritants or cause allergies. Pollen allergies, or hay fever, are caused by a small number of plants (grasses, weeds, and specific tree species) that depend on wind for cross-pollination. The American Medical Association (AMA) Guide is a good source of information, and many poison-control centers publish information on native poisonous and non-poisonous plants. Insect bites, particularly bee stings, can cause allergic reactions. Without consultation with medical practitioners, it can be difficult for designers to evaluate the danger of bee stings and flea, spider, tick and mosquito bites. A perceived threat, from a bee for example, will often undermine the use of the garden and can be as limiting as a real threat.

## 4.2. Design considerations and recommendations

Design considerations, while general in nature, make good planning guidelines and can form the core of the design concept. This is often a new and valuable concept for staff and stresses the idea that the site is unique and each resident is an individual—with individual needs, abilities, and perceptions. Design efforts should reflect this sensitivity for both site and resident, while acknowledging the opportunities and constraints in each in order to create a fully engaging experience. The following is a representative outline of general design parameters.

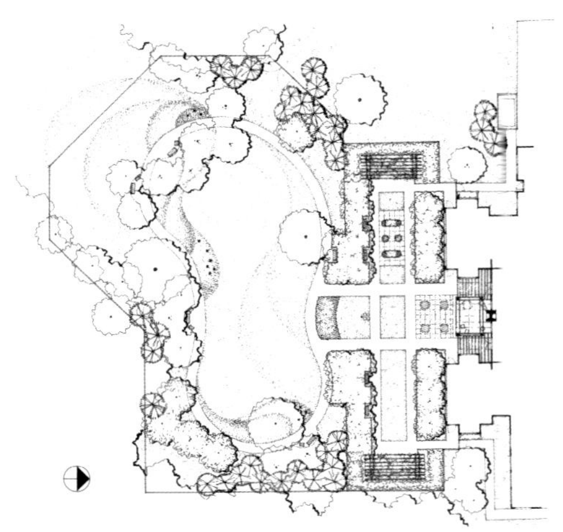

◂ Garden design plan

The Design Plan articulates the Concept Plan with specific details.

### 4.2.1. Diversity in site design

Gardens should contain areas that offer aesthetic and functional variety and accommodate a range of uses. The overall organization should be easily identified and understood, to provide comfort and security—both real and perceived. Engaging outdoor spaces offer a variety of distinct settings with opportunities for observation or activity and varying levels of participation. For example, one area might provide a sunny and lively setting for group activities—with nearby seating for residents to observe without participating. Another area might provide a calm, intimate setting in dappled shade for more private moments. If space permits, consider areas with varying levels of sensory stimulation. Some spaces might be filled with color and fragrance; others might be calm shades of green.

### 4.2.2. Accessibility, ease of use, and safety

Gardens must be easily and safely accessible, accommodating individuals with varied and changing interests, abilities, and needs. Mobility throughout the garden is achieved by providing spaces that are easy to enter, move through, and exit. Such mobility allows for the convenient use and enjoyment of all features within the garden. Safety considerations include careful plant selection. Avoid plants that create hazardous conditions such as those that are poisonous, thorny, or scratchy; cause allergies or itchiness; or produce messy or slippery droppings of sap, pods, fruit or leaves. Consider root structure in tree selections. Avoid trees with surface roots that can cause unevenness in adjacent paths and paving.

### 4.2.3. Diversity of plant material

Plants should be selected to provide a variety of sensory interests, including seasonal changes of colors and fragrances, form, textures, and tastes. Use plants to demarcate spaces and displays, and provide screening and shelter. Plant selection and arrangement should maximize interest, provide opportunities for participation at a variety of levels, and reflect desired maintenance levels and security requirements. Plant selections might emphasize familiar local landscapes, including farmland, woodlands, and meadows. Trees and shrubs can frame seasonally interesting views of the garden from resident windows while also providing a sense of privacy from views within the garden.

### 4.2.4. Quality of maintenance

Gardens will remain attractive, safe, and functional only if properly maintained. Recognize the garden's realistic and ongoing maintenance needs and provide sufficient funds for staff, training, supplies, and equipment. A rich and diverse planting design need not require intensive maintenance. Designs with low maintenance costs, however, do require careful attention to the initial material selection and coordination with operational procedures. Maintain a 7-foot (2.1-meter) branching height for trees adjacent to pathways; other trees might be lower branched for privacy, interest and attracting birdlife. To create a more relaxed garden ambiance and also attract birdlife, allow shrubs to achieve their natural, open branching habit and form, minimizing the heavily pruned/dense appearance.

## 4.3. Refining the design considerations

These planning guidelines can form the basis for more detailed discussions on materials, details and programs, including the following:

- **Inclusive programming**

If a garden is being planned, consider involving both residents and staff in the programming. Will residents be able to see the garden from their rooms or apartments? Many seniors grew vegetables in their more active years and have fond memories of vegetable gardens. Vegetable gardens can often be major topics of interest and conversation for residents. If the garden is properly placed, they can watch the growth of herbs, fruits, and vegetables from inside and be encouraged to participate. Weekly harvests can become opportunities for social activities involving fresh garden produce, and end-of-season harvest celebrations can become important events for residents, families, and staff.

- **Activity areas**

The design of group activity areas must consider the number and types of participants in wheelchairs and others who may need assistance with helpers, or other aids. The design must account for the schedule of activities, storage, carting, and use of materials and equipment. Porches are convenient activity areas with easy access to interior spaces. They should be spacious and provide flexible areas for active and passive uses and clear circulation to and from the garden with minimal disruption or distraction. Circulation to, from, and through activity areas should establish clear destinations and, typically, form a series of looped routes, returning to the main entrance, or other landmark.

- **Specialized activity areas**

When planning for programs such as horticultural therapy, it is important to determine how many people will be involved in an activity. Part of the value of horticultural therapy comes from developing a relationship between the resident and horticultural

◢ Garden design section

Emphasizing the original concept of a progression of spaces, this section conveys the idea of spaces increasing in size, height of overhead canopy, and exposure to the elements. Graphic studies such as this help the project team to visualize and articulate the desired goals of the garden.

therapist. When groups become larger than 10, the setting is rarely intimate. If you are working with 10 residents, you must also consider how many supportive people, both caregivers and volunteers, will need to be involved for the experience to be meaningful. The required number of supportive people depends upon the physical, emotional and developmental makeup of the group. For example, it is possible to have six clients and need six support staff and/or caregivers, requiring careful consideration in the available area for horticultural activities.

- **Paving**

Physical limitations must be carefully considered when determining the width of pathways and their gradients, materials used in construction, and seating and cues for the vision impaired. Paving materials should be secure with sufficient texture to ensure a firm feel underfoot and minimize slipping, but not too textured to exhaust garden visitors with limited stamina and those who shuffle their feet while walking. Materials must be low-glare to accommodate individual abilities in adjusting to varying light levels. This is particularly important in the transition between indoor and outdoor spaces, under tree canopies and under garden structures. Avoid strong sun/shade contrasts as they create confusing patterns. Pavement gradients should provide for proper drainage to avoid water collecting on walking surfaces (approximately 2 percent) but be minimal to prevent walkers and wheelchairs from veering off the desired direction.

- **Specialized paving**

There is an opportunity to introduce specialized areas with more challenging paving surfaces and gradients into the garden setting. Gardens offer an excellent resource for occupational and physical therapists and to introduce familiar 'everyday' scenarios into their therapeutic regimen. This might include varying paving surfaces (brick, cobble, stonedust, and so on) as well as steeper pathways, ramps and steps, and other outdoor routines, such as mailboxes. In close collaboration with staff, introduce a sense of challenge and adventure into the garden experience.

- **Raised beds, planters, and garden amenities**

Plant beds that are raised to accommodate individual preferences to sit, stand or stoop can expand participation in garden activities. Consider varying planter heights in 10-centimeter (4-inch) increments from 60 centimeters (24 inches) to 90 centimeters (36 inches). Raised beds can have indented toe spaces so residents can be closer to the work area. Large planters can encourage socialization with two or three residents in wheelchairs, or those sitting in chairs can easily work with plants. And don't forget the plants themselves: Is there adequate sunshine for plant growth? Window boxes secured to porch rails with paved surfaces on both sides provide added opportunities for socialization. Tools and materials should be stored near activity areas for easy access and to emphasize a familiar, homelike ambiance (such as a garden shed). Bird feeders, rain gauges and other amenities such as a flagpole or hanging baskets can build upon familiar daily routines while creating opportunities for exercise and improving motor-coordination skills.

- **Garden furniture**

Bench and chair selections should be based upon their sturdiness, beauty, and the height of seats, which relates to ease of seating. While both chairs and benches should be offered in the garden chairs can be easier for an aging person to use. Benches should be wide enough for two individuals to sit comfortably together for conversation. Consider tables that expand for varying group sizes and that accommodate umbrellas if needed. Wood is a typical material for its softness to the touch, weight, and warmth (particularly in colder climates) as compared to the cold touch of metal. Consider nearby water-protected storage for cushions. Chairs should have sturdy arms, which can be used to help a person rise, and the chair width large enough to accommodate someone of generous proportions. Chairs offer valuable flexibility and choice in placement—as impromptu settings for group or individual use, privacy, or easily moved to capture sun or shade for individual comfort.

- **Fencing and gates**

Careful consideration must be given to the garden's enclosure, ensuring a safe and secure setting while also preventing a sense of confinement, and the frequent resultant feelings of frustration, agitation, and confusion. Depending upon the desires of the staff, both solid and open-view fencing might be used to achieve specific goals. For example, open fencing offers a sense of 'beyond' to an adjacent natural setting, and solid fencing blocks views of undesirable activities. Strategically placed plant materials and even grade changes can mitigate the prominence of the garden's edge and fencing, but carefully determine grade heights and select plant varieties that maintain clear views for staff monitoring. Garden amenities and plant displays can be placed 'inward' of the fence to focus attention inside the garden. Secured gates can be placed outside the general view while providing easy access for maintenance and special events.

- **Water**

Water is a major factor to consider when creating a garden. Watering plants can be good exercise for certain populations. Providing short hoses that aging people can manipulate easily can lessen the potential tripping problems inherent in using long lengths of hose for watering. For some aging people, using a watering can provides opportunities for exercise that can improve upper-body movements while allowing several people to water at the same time. Not only is water needed for the plants, but water is required for clients to drink and to wash hands after activities; this should be considered when planning a garden.

- Discovery

Finally, consider the experiences of first-time residents and visitors, and encourage their 'discovery' of the garden by creating clear, identifiable interior signage and other wayfinding strategies. Introduce small display areas within the facility that highlight garden activities or feature 'what is in bloom' to encourage the garden's exploration and enjoyment.

# 5/ Gardens for People with Dementia

Author: Kim Grove
Garden designer

From 'Gardens for People with Dementia: A guide to make them safe and suitable', published January 2012.

## 5.1. Introduction

Most people living with dementia live either at home or in a care home, and so many will have access to a garden. A garden is a place where a person with dementia can engage in familiar, memorable activities such as planting and digging, growing flowers or vegetables, cutting flowers to bring indoors, hanging out the washing, walking around the garden or sitting, relaxing and enjoying the natural sounds the garden makes. Research shows us that natural elements—such as plants (including flowers), sunshine, water, birds and animals, and fragrance—can make us feel better by reducing stress, reducing blood pressure, and helping us to achieve an overall sense of well-being. It therefore follows that gardens are places of great therapeutic value. Just being in the garden provides much-needed fresh air, giving the brain a boost of oxygen, which can be hard to come by indoors when we tend to breathe in the same air over and again. Carrying out gardening activities—such as walking round the garden, deadheading roses, hanging out the washing, or growing vegetables or flowers—assists the person to take a little more exercise than they might otherwise. Exercise is known to reduce stress and depression, and can help to lower anxiety. Sunlight is a great source of Vitamin D so small amounts of exposure to the sun (10–20 minutes) each day, particularly in spring and summer, can help the body produce more of this. Vitamin D helps to keep our bones healthy, and is important for people with dementia as it helps to fight depression. However, care must be taken to ensure there is no over-exposure to the sun. The garden can be a place of peace and quiet, which can help to ease stress, anxiety, agitation, aggressive behavior, and pain—all of which people with dementia can experience.

For an outdoor space to provide therapeutic benefit to residents and service users with dementia, certain requirements must be met in terms of the layout, circulation, elements, and features. It is an advantage to consider the location and position of the building in the early stages of planning or renovating your site, as the indoor–outdoor connection will affect the actual use of the garden and therefore its therapeutic potential. Beyond the physical requirements, a beneficial connection to nature must be facilitated more broadly by involving staff, families, friends, and volunteers in the ongoing use of the space.

## 5.2. Design considerations and recommendations

Author: Chalfont Design
From the 'Dementia Green Care Design Guide', published 2012.
(http://www.chalfontdesign.com/media/Design_Guide.pdf)

### 5.2.1 Support and enable people into movement and activity

Care environments are becoming increasingly complex in terms of the diversity of needs and abilities they must support. Consider areas for both active use (stimulates and enables active participation) and passive use (supplies entertainment or respite). Different areas can be designed to accommodate each. Likewise, some people will want to use the garden independently, while others need to be supported and encouraged. Obviously a wide range of uses requires attention be paid to safety and risk. But one size does not fit all and it will actually erode the therapeutic benefits you are aiming for. A wide range of needs and abilities calls for different areas to be separated but integrated.

### 5.2.2. Passive space

A passive space is one that encourages calm restfulness, where residents can enjoy some peace and quiet, a sense of freedom, some fresh air and a chance to get away from other residents. One type of passive space is a sitting-out space. It should be a comfortable seat or seating area that residents can go to and use on their own. The person passively receives stimulation from the natural world, so plants and daylight must be abundant. Green is the most calming color, but blue and white blossoms will add to the restful effect. The sound of water can be added with a water feature that gives an audible quality to the space.

Passive space has certain qualities that support a therapeutic experience:

- Comfortable furniture to encourage resting surrounded by sensory nature.
- Peaceful views to help a person calm down and relax.
- A glimpse of wildlife encouraged by the nearness of a tree, bird bath, or bird feeder.
- Enclosure or shelter—an arbor seat or a structure with seating, a roof, and a view out.
- Trees, shrubs, and flowering plants to interest and delight.

### 5.2.3. Active space

To encourage an active lifestyle for people with dementia in a care setting, promote movement and activity by including these aspirations in the design brief:

- Enables frequent trips outdoors for fresh air, sunshine, and connection to nature.
- Enables people to be actively engaged outdoors in a variety of ways.
- Enables safe movement by accommodating physical and perceptual limitations.
- Offers opportunities for staff to calm, distract, and redirect interest (such as 'a sensory stroll').
- Supports activities that can be recorded, measured, and compared to resident outcomes.

To create active space, these therapeutic activities need to be enabled through design:

- Feeding, exercising, petting or caring for animals.
- Starting and tending to seeds and plants.
- Doing 'proper jobs', such as mowing, raking and sweeping, or hanging out laundry.
- Frequent or routine involvement in useful, meaningful garden work.
- Harvesting fruit, vegetables, herbs, and flowers for cooking or decorating inside the home.
- Playing with racquets, bats, golf clubs, and balls (swing, hit, aim, catch, kick, or throw).
- Exercise, sports or green gym (for aerobic exercise, repetitive movement, balance, coordination, and use of strength).
- Playing on playground equipment (choose items that kids of all ages can enjoy).

### 5.2.4. Risk-free and risk-assumed gardens

The concept of a risk-free garden or a risk-assumed garden avoids the fate of many care-home gardens that are so low-risk they are useless therapeutically. This concept prevents all outdoor spaces in the home from being designed with the lowest possible expectation for resident involvement.

#### Risk-free gardens

Risk-free gardens are outdoor areas that a resident with dementia, even with distressed behavior, could use independently. This space is of special value to residents who are physically able, highly mobile, and walk constantly. These gardens need to be visible from indoor rooms so staff can see people using them. A balcony is an example of a risk-free garden as residents will be able to access it when they want. A risk-free garden would have an open-door policy. The following design criteria apply:

- For rapid movement and limitations in spatial awareness, make path surfaces uniform in width, color and texture.
- If a poured surface is used, ensure proper fall lines so there is no standing water on the path. Also make the final surface texture not too smooth (slippery) and not too rough (friction).
- Make no sharp turns in the path that would allow a person to walk off the path into a bed.
- Turns or curves require the addition of a handrail or, better yet, use a structure to guide people along the path, like the edge of a raised bed, a section of picket fence or the back of a bench.
- Furniture is largely 'fixed' and static; moveable furniture is heavy and robust, making it difficult to push over.

- Pots and planters are a size and height to be clearly visible to a person while walking quickly. (Anything lower than the waist will not be seen and may be walked into or tripped over).
- No structures are to be placed against the perimeter fence if they could be used to climb on (such as raised beds and benches).
- If they enclose space, trellises are to be diagonal with small holes (impossible to climb)
- Create no ambiguous openings a person may try to squeeze through—make them large enough to walk through or close them off.
- Don't use plants with prickles or thorns and nothing poisonous.
- Use toughened safety glass for windows in a shed, greenhouse, summer house, or potting shed.
- Don't use water bodies (such as ponds and fountains with a water surface and depth of water).
- Create a lawn that is flat and level with no curbing or upstands between the lawn and the beds.
- A continuous path should lead away from the door and return either to that door or some other way back inside.
- Allow for visibility from inside windows of the home. Make sure people outside can be easily seen from indoors, even when in a workshop, gazebo, or other structure. Consider placement of windows in these structures for sun and visibility, both into and out of them.

## Risk-assumed gardens

Risk-assumed gardens are outdoor areas that a resident with dementia will only use when accompanied by a responsible person. These are the key characteristics or design criteria:

- Part of the garden (perhaps all of it) may not be visible from indoor rooms.
- It is intended as a special destination that will enhance and extend family visits by providing areas with meaning and purpose.
- This is where much of the therapeutic activity will happen between staff and residents. 'Family Garden' is the name used to identify an area that is risk-assumed because it will be frequented by families and will include all-ages play equipment.

## 5.2.5. Courtyard gardens

As these are visible from internal rooms, and because an internal courtyard is an enclosed space, they should at least be 'Risk-Free', with an open-door policy for residents to access the space unassisted. Depending on the home's ability to facilitate engagement, to know and understand the residents, and to manage the risk, a courtyard can also have some 'Risk-assumed' items such as water features, a glider or swing seat, and a piece of exercise equipment.

Here are two examples of a courtyard garden visible from indoor rooms:

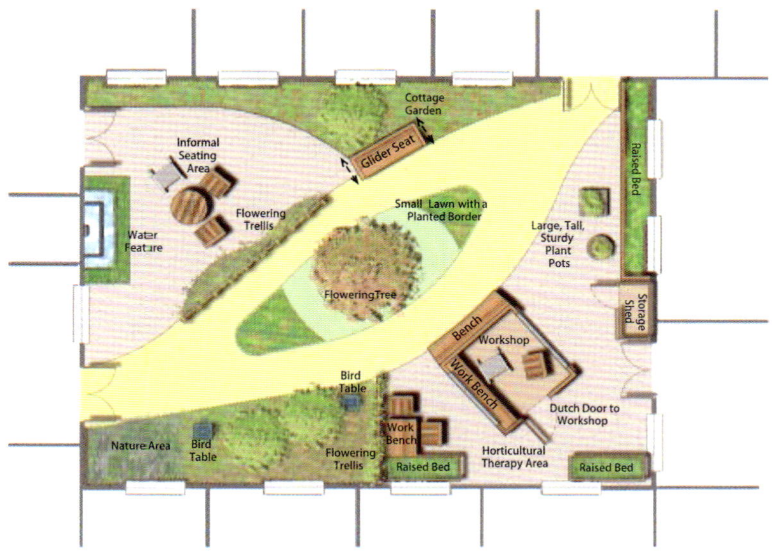


### Example 1—Courtyard garden (Risk-assumed)

This courtyard space has a central lawn with a planted border of fragrant, colorful plants. It acts as the focal point to the main access paths from the building, providing a zone for active movement. The central flowering tree anchors the space, and gives residents interesting seasonal experiences both from inside the building and from within the courtyard. An informal seating area in close proximity to a water feature will create a space where residents can sit, and enjoy the sensory qualities of water. Planted edges to the courtyard provide not only a privacy buffer to the interior spaces, but also make the courtyard into a pleasant green garden, with planting variety. Trellis arrangements provide a variance in height to the structure of the space, a place for flowering climbers to grow, and places where people can sit and feel protected. The horticultural therapy area is a place where residents can undertake activities and have ownership of their courtyard garden.

### Example 2—Courtyard garden (Risk-free)

Block paving provides a safe, smooth, non-slip walking surface throughout. Areas of sun and shade are provided for use by

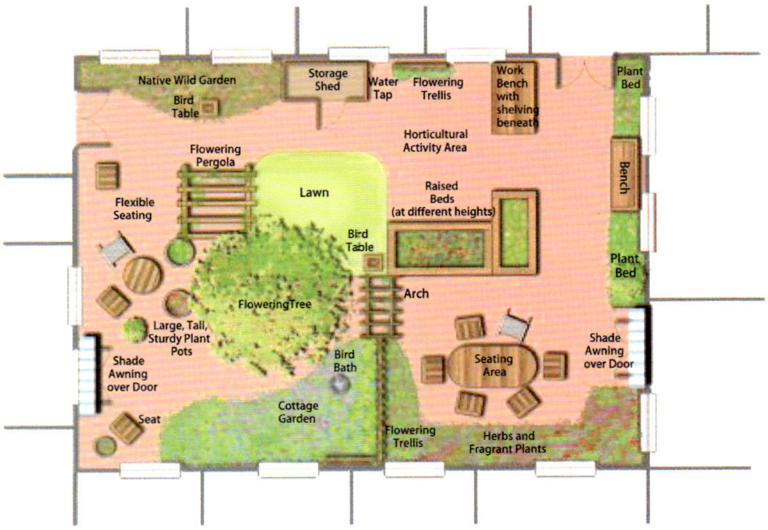


individuals, couples, or groups. Plantings include edible plants, vegetables, traditional cottage garden plants as well as native plants, trailing vines, herbs, fragrant plants, and colorful annuals. A garden work area contains a workbench and a shed for organized horticultural activities or simply pottering about. Raised beds, tall pots and trellises bring plants within reach. Diverse plantings add color and fragrance to trigger memories, provide meaningful occupation, stimulate the senses, and lift the spirit. Wildlife is encouraged by providing food, forage, shelter, and perches with the native wild area, pergola, arch, tree, trellises, and bird feeders. Awnings provide shade on the sunny side of the space.

### 5.2.6. Design criteria to promote activity in a therapeutic garden

1. Potting shed, workshop (or a bespoke combination of the two), or a purpose-built poly-tunnel for doing garden projects, planting up, woodwork, or tinkering with tools.
2. Tool stores, cabinets and equipment storage for tools, games, cushions, and so on, to encourage people to use the outdoors. Familiar things to carry, push or kick give meaning and purpose to the movement.
3. Electric outlets in the workshop for power tools, lights, a radio, a heater, a kettle, and so on, to make the place usable and comfortable (the Shed Therapy approach).
4. A lawn area useful for play and games, sports, grass cutting, building snowmen, and so on.
5. Wildlife area with habitat plants, feeders, bird tables, nesting boxes, and a bug hotel.
6. Water taps and/or a water butt for watering plants, topping up the water feature, and cleaning and refilling the bird baths.
7. Different types of fencing and trellis to support hanging baskets, bird feeders, silly signs, and decorative elements. All joinery should be comfortable to the touch and sanded smooth, then preserved with paint, stain, or oil. The joiner can advise on what to use for which wood and the maintenance required.
8. Horticultural activity spaces for small groups or one-to-one work in a focused space.

The table to the right shows garden features that can be made safe and used in a risk-free garden.

| Garden feature | Adaption for use in a risk-free garden |
|---|---|
| Potting shed or workshop | • Put windows on three sides and a door on the fourth side with a window in it.<br>• Position the structure where it can be seen from inside the home. |
| Shed | • If contents are harmless (chicken feed, straw, bird feed, soil, pots, and so on.) then put the shed where it can be seen from inside the home and leave it unlocked.<br>• If it contains tools, keep locked and use when staff are outside with residents. |
| Water feature | • Use the bubbler type with water flowing over a stone and gurgling down through small rocks into an enclosed reservoir. There is no water surface in this type.<br>• To have a water surface so the fountain actually makes a splashing sound, you can fit a metal grate to span across the water surface of a pond, just a couple of inches below the surface. This is easier to build if the pond is square or round and has solid walls (brick or concrete). The grate prevents someone falling in. |
| Pots, planters and ornaments | • Small low pots, planters and ornaments in a normal garden can be tripping hazards if a person does not see them in time to avoid them. Such items can be placed against a wall or in a planting bed.<br>• For pots in the paved areas, use large, tall, sturdy pots (can be round or square) that are table height, easier for people to plant and highly visible. |
| Pergola, trellis, arch or tree | • Any person in a care environment would struggle to take their own life but it is still possible. A pergola, trellis, arch or tree will have what are called 'ligature points' and hence they are often ruled out in clinical/hospital mental health settings. For people with dementia and distressed behaviour these structures could still be lethal if a person is intent on suicide. But a garden with no vertical structures or trees is lethal to the soul. So do not rule them out altogether. Instead, use these structures in garden areas visible from indoors. Most importantly, know your residents. If anybody is at risk of self-harm, go outside with them until they are no longer at risk of injuring themselves. Structures can also be designed ligature-free. |

# 6/ Hospice Gardens

Author: Charles King Sadler
Landscape designer
From, Design Guidelines for Effective Hospice Gardens Using Japanese Garden Principles, published January, 2007.

## 6.1. Introduction

The modern hospice-movement's mission is to provide palliative care, which includes pain and symptom management, to people who are expected to live six months or less. This is a very different mission from other health-care facilities where the goal is curative care. No curative treatment is given to hospice patients currently. Hospice gardens have a more specific program than some health-care garden design, such as acute-care hospitals that deals with many types of patients and have a more open-ended program. Hospice gardens have a specific patient group with specific requirements. A successful hospice garden creates a safe and welcoming environment, full of vegetation for the patients, family, and staff to enjoy. By following the properties of being away, extent, fascination, and compatibility, the garden clears ones mind and allows a restorative experience to take place, thus reducing anxiety and tension. A familiar landscape is important in hospice gardens as it is comforting at the end of life. The familiar is comforting and reassuring, especially for emotionally strained patients. Using native plants and recreating patterns seen in the regional landscape can help to create this familiar landscape.

In a hospice garden the family members are the primary garden users. A secluded spot for the family will allow for quiet prayer and meditation; slowly moving or still water can also facilitate this activity. The staff are the second-most frequent users of the garden so it is important for them to have a private area, separate from the families, in which they can relax and let their minds wander, thereby alleviating work-related stress. It is also important that the staff can view the garden while working indoors. It is vital that the garden be visible to the patients while in bed, since this may be the closest they get to the garden on many days. At the end of life, individuals are particularly sensitive to cold, heat, and wind. A shielded outdoor area or covered veranda, will extend the use of the garden; protection from wind, rain and sun will allow frail patients more use of the outdoor space. While it is important to use recognizable plants so the garden is familiar, an occasional unique specimen plant can add wonder and fascination. Since the patients will view the garden primarily from inside, it is essential the landscape have year-round interest. Choosing plants that attract select wildlife, such as birds or butterflies, can add value and interest to the garden. Thoughtful plant selection will keep the flora intriguing in all four seasons. The use of some evergreen plants will aid sustained winter interest. In addition to plants, secondary elements such as water features, chimes, and bird feeders can help animate the garden with life and bring sound to the patients, family members and staff both inside and outdoors

### 6.1.1. General hospice garden guidelines

1. Provide transitional spaces between indoor and outdoor spaces to allow adjustment to bright outdoor light.
2. Provide soothing natural sounds in the garden, as hearing is often the last of the senses to leave a dying person.
3. Provide quiet places to sit and contemplate.
4. Encourage people to touch things in the garden, use plants and structures with a variety of textures.
5. Provide a view from the window for patients that can't go outside.
6. Design with materials that improve, rather than wear out, with age.
7. Provide a water feature. Water is a soothing agent. Still water can provide a setting for meditation or prayer while the sound of and view of moving water is undeniably restorative.

## 6.2. Design considerations and recommendations

### 6.2.1 Front garden

The circulation patterns immediately around the building are well constructed and allow for seating of both ambulatory individuals and wheelchair-bound individuals. The front garden, which faces the street, is rich in plant material having four-season interest, contains an interesting water feature, and provides various seating options. Space is allowed for wheelchair mobility in and through this section of the garden. This garden has some indoor/outdoor connection, but fails to sufficiently tie the garden to the interior, with some plant material obstructing the view from indoors. The road is sufficiently screened from view and the site offers a sense of extent from its abundant plantings and layered views. Thoughtful consideration of plant material makes this garden pleasing year-round.

### 6.2.2. Side garden

The side garden links the front and rear garden areas. Aesthetically this area is successful, but functionally the paved circulation path abruptly ends, due to erosion of the stone dust and timber path, creating an uneven grade and making wheelchair travel difficult. An integrated hierarchical circulation system is needed, so that wheelchairs can navigate easily through the majority of the garden. Secondary paths that are not ADA accessible can offer other options, as long as no paths dead-end, leaving the mobility-challenged individual with no options. A secluded area exists in the side garden; this private area is ideal for quiet prayer and meditation for the resident or family members, or as a refuge for staff. A rock garden area allows for various seating option on boulders and interesting and varied plant material.

### 6.2.3. Rear garden

The grade drops about one story as it rounds the building to the rear so this area is surrounded on two sides by a two-story building. This area offers some play options for children and various seating options. A fish-bowl effect is caused by the extensive windows that face this area, while there is little plant material to screen the garden users. This may be the weakest area of the site due to this fact. More evergreen plant material would strengthen this area and provide more winter interest. A second-floor veranda allows residents to view the garden from their rooms through large sliding glass doors; wind chimes and hanging plants add visual interest for residents. The railing obstructs some of the view from a seated position (wheelchair). The semi-protected veranda offers great garden viewing for patients during mild weather.

### 6.2.4. Pond area

This area lacks much shade or wind protection, which are vital for frail, infirm residents. The 2-acre (8094-square-meter) pond and surrounding area offer a welcome contrast to the mowed and landscape area around the residence. One feels compatible with this apparently wild unmowed and wooded section of the property. Some seating is available and wildlife viewing, especially waterfowl, can be enjoyed from the picnic-table area. A circular path leads one around the pond allowing for restoration from nature to occur, however, this dirt path would be difficult to navigate with a wheelchair.

### 6.2.5. Site selection criteria and process

1. It is essential that the patient, family, and staff areas of the hospice face the garden for restoration to occur.
2. In order for all patients to have easy physical access to the garden and the hospice in general, the building should be ADA accessible and have patients primarily on the first floor.
3. The first floor is best for intimate garden views.
4. Finally, the hospice staff and administrators will be the contacts for the author's study, it is important that the staff is friendly and helpful for this design study to make progress and be successful.

### 6.2.6. Desirable hospice garden guidelines

1. Ensure familiar building and garden design; nothing strange or challenging at end of life.
2. Provide variety of walking routes.
3. Create hierarchy of pathways: for wheelchair use and lone exploration on foot. Avoid dead-end, wheelchair-accessible paths.
4. Meandering pathways provide changing viewpoints, and a sense of getting away.
5. Create destination points.
6. Create a series of 'outdoor rooms' for a sense of exploration and arrival.
7. Choose a predominance of plants familiar in the culture, and a lot of variety.
8. Add occasional unfamiliar accent plants, which may trigger conversation.
9. Provide moveable and fixed garden furniture.
10. Create settings (a secret path or bench) where a person can be alone.
11. Provide places for families to meet in private
12. Create features in the garden that will extend its use throughout the year, such as a covered outdoor area with protection from the wind and sun.
13. Provide soothing sounds: water, birdsong, rustling leaves, and chimes. It is important for these sounds to be heard in the rooms, especially the sound of moving water.
14. Incorporate unambiguous positive sculpture (representational artwork).
15. Create viewpoints where topography permits.
16. Ensure all rooms have green (garden or nature) outlook, and that the landscaping is appealing all year round.
17. Provide restorative environments for the staff, both in the gardens and indoor areas with garden views.
18. Provide distractions for visiting children, such as play areas or sand boxes.
19. Create low-key designs for donor recognition, but avoid plaques that say 'In memory of...' beside each tree, as these can remind patients and families of death.

# References


## 1. Healing Garden

Brown, T., McLafferty, S., Moon, G., 2010, *A Companion to: Health and Medical Geography*, Blackwell Publishing Ltd.

Franke, T. T., 1996, 'Making Future Landscapes: Defining a Path to Qualified Sustainability', *Landurbplan*, vol. 35, pp. 241–6.

Marcus, Clare Cooper and Marni Barnes (eds), 1999, *Healing Gardens: Therapeutic Benefits and Design*, John Wiley and Sons, New York.

Morse, S., Vogiatzakis, I., Griffiths, G., 2011, Space and Sustainability. Potential for Landscape a Spatial Unit for Assessing Sustainability', *Sustainable Development*, vol. 19, pp. 30–48.

Rawlings, R., 1998, *Healing Gardens: Aromatherapy – Feng Shui – Holistic Gardening – Herbalism – Color Therapy – Meditation*. Willow Creek Press, USA.

Stark, A., 2004, *Creating Outstanding Environments with Geomancy and Feng Shui: Guidelines for Healing Gardens*, http://www.alexstark.com.

Stigsdotter, U. A., 2005, *Landscape Architecture and Health: Evidence-Based Health-Promoting Design and Planning*. Doctoral thesis, Department of Landscape Planning Alnarp, Swedish University of Agricultural Science.

Vapaa, A. G., 2002, *Healing Gardens: Creating Places for Restoration, Meditation and Sanctuary: What are Defining Characteristics that Make a Healing Garden?*, Masters thesis, College of Architecture and Urban Studies, Virginia Polytechnic Institute and State University.

## 2. Healthcare Center Outdoor Landscape

Allison, David, 2007, 'Hospital as City', *Health Facilities Management Magazine*, http://www.hfmmagazine.com/hfmmagazine/jsp/articledisplay.jsp?dcrpath=hfmmagazine/article/data/06jun2007/0706hfm_dept_arch_design & domain=hfmmagazine, (accessed January 2013).

American Planning Association, 2012, *Planning and Urban Design Standards*, John Wiley & Sons, Hoboken, NJ USA.

Department of Veterans Affairs, 2010, *Mental Health Facilities Design Guide*, www.cfm.va.gov/til/dguide/dgmh.pdf (accessed January 2013).

Epstein Mark, 2006, 'Hospital Gardens Help Patients Heal', *Seattle Daily Journal Health Care Design & Construction*, vol. 11.

Fang, Eric C.Y., 2000, *The Hospital and the City*, International Academy for Design and Health.

Franklin, Deborah, 2012, 'How Hospital Gardens Help Patients Heal', *Scientific American Magazine*, vol. 3.

Furgeson, Molly, 2012, *Healing Gardens*, Department of Horticultural Science, University of Minnesota, http://www.sustland.umn.edu/design/healinggardens.html (accessed January 2013).

Gerlach-Spriggs, Nancy, Richard Enoch Kaufman and Sam Bass Warner, Jr., 2004, *Restorative Gardens*, Yale University Press, New Haven and London.

Gupta, Kant and Shakti Kuma Gupta, 2007, *Modern Trends in Planning and Designing of Hospitals: Principles and Practice*, Jaypee Brothers.

International Parking Institute, 2009, 'Hospital Parking: A Proactive Approach for Managing', *The Parking Professional Magazine*, October, pp. 33–5.

Kaplan, R. and S. Kaplan, 1983, *Cognition and Environment: Functioning in an Uncertain World*, New York, Praeger.

Kunders, G.D., 2008, *Hospitals: Facilities Planning and Management*, Tata McGraw-Hill Education.

Leibrock, Cynthia A. and Debra Harris, 2011, *Design Details for Health: Making the Most of Design's Healing Potential*, 2nd edn, John Wiley & Sons, New York.

Main, Bill and Gail Greet Hannah, 2010, *Site Furnishings: A Complete Guide to the Planning, Selection and Use of Landscape Furniture and Amenities*, John Wiley & Sons, USA.

Marcus, Clare Cooper, 2010, *Landscape Design: Patient-Specific Healing Gardens*, World Health Design, http://www.worldhealthdesign.com/patient-specific-healing-gardens.aspx (accessed January 2013).

Marcus, Clare Cooper, 2002, *Gardens and Health*, International Academy for Design and Health.

Marcus, Clare Cooper and Marni Barnes, 1995, *Gardens in Healthcare Facilities: Uses Therapeutic Benefits, and Design Recommendations*, The Center for Health Design, Inc.

Marcus, Clare Cooper and Carolyn Francis, 1997, *People Places: Design Guidelines for Urban Open Space*, John Wiley & Sons.

Neducin, Dejana, Milena Krklješ and Nađa Kurović-Folić, 2010, 'Hospital Outdoor Spaces: Therapeutic Benefits and Design Considerations' *Facta Universitatis Series: Architecture and Civil Engineering*, vol. 8, no. 3, pp. 293–305.

NHS Estates, 2005, *Wayfinding, Effective Wayfinding and Signing Systems, Guidance for Healthcare Facilities*, 2nd edn, Stationery Office Books.

Nord, R. Del., 2009, *The Culture for the Future of Healthcare Architecture*, proceedings of the 28th International Public Health Seminar.

Parcell, Stacy, 2012, 'Healing Garden's New Dimension: Edible Gardens', *Healthcare Design Magazine*, vol. 5, Chicago.

Piotrowsk, Christine M., 2007, *Designing Commercial Interiors*, Wiley.

Queensland Health, 1999, *Design Guidelines for Queensland Aged Care Facilities*, http://www.health.qld.gov.au/cwamb/agedguide/13037.pdf (accessed January 2013).

Sadler, Charles King, 2007, *Design Guidelines for Effective Hospice Gardens Using Japanese Garden Principles*, Masters thesis, Faculty of Landscape Architecture Suny College of Environmental Sciences and Forestry, Syracuse, New York.

Schucker, Robert, 2010, *Hospitals Adding Rooftop Gardens to Improve Patient Care*, www.beckershospitalreview.com/news-analysis/hospitals-adding-roof-gardens-to-improve-patient-care.html (accessed January 2013).

Severtsen, Betsy, 2006, 'Healing Gardens', *Gardens*, vol. 3, http://www.majorfoundation.org/campaign-for-the-beautiful.htm (accessed January 2013).

Shackell, Aileen and Robin Walter, 2012, *Practice Guide Greenspace Design for Health and Well Being*, Forestry Commission, Edinburgh.

Shepley, M. McCuskey, 2006, 'The Role of Positive Distraction in Neonatal Intensive Care Unit Settings' *Journal of Perinatology*, vol. 26, pp. 34–7.

Smith, Jerry, 2007, *Health and Nature: The Influence of Nature on Design of the Environment of Care*, The Center for Health Design, http://www.healthdesign.org/chd/research/health-and-nature-influence-nature-design-environment-care (accessed January 2013).

Ulrich, R. S., 2002, *Health Benefits of Gardens in Hospitals*, Plants for People Conference, International Exhibition Floriade.

Ulrich, R. S., 1984, 'View Through a Window May Influence Recovery from Surgery', *Science*, vol. 224, no. 4647, pp. 420–1.

Vapaa, Annalisa Gartman, 2002, *Healing Gardens: Creating Places for Restoration, Meditation, and Sanctuary, What Are the Defining Characteristics That make a Healing Garden?* Masters thesis, Virginia Polytechnic Institute and State University College of Architecture and Urban Studies.

Verderber, Stephen and Ben J. Refuerzo, 2006, *Innovations in Hospice Architecture*, Taylor & Francis.

# Eskenazi Health Hospital's Healing Waters & Falls Fountains

LOCATION
Indianapolis, USA

AREA
1367.01 square feet (172 square meters)

CLIENT
Eskenazi Health Hospital

COMPLETION DATE
2014

LANDSCAPE DESIGN
LAND COLLECTIVE, David Rubin, Principal

FOUNTAIN DESIGNER
Fluidity Design Consultants,
Jim Garland, Principal

BUDGET
US$1 million

PHOTOGRAPHY
Sahar Coston-Hardy

BLUEPRINT

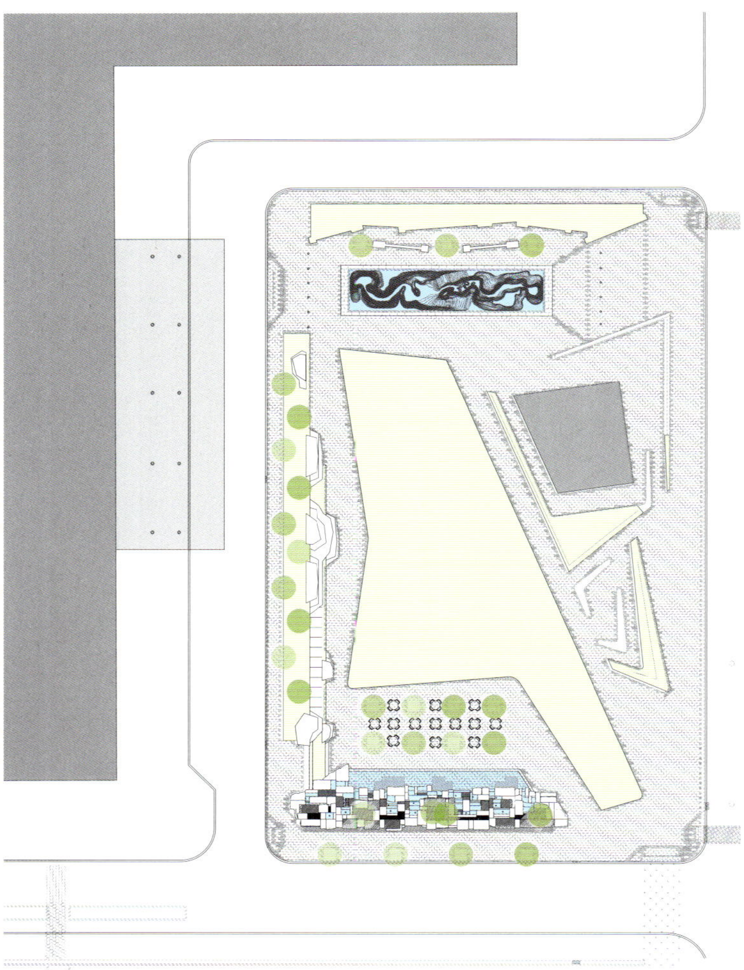

Project site plan

It is valuable to recognize that this garden was planned by the hospital and its designers to function as a social space for the community, integrated into the fabric of Indianapolis in a gesture of public outreach, and meaningfully embracing dual themes of health and healing. The garden planners were motivated by the nature of the hospital's clientele who are mostly underprivileged people, and whom it is believed would benefit from the hospital's energetic advocacy of healthy lifestyles. Such an exceedingly moral idea might easily have led to a terribly boring garden. The wonderful place that was created involved both skill and mystery.

Two relatively large water features, each very different from the other in character and purpose, contribute to the garden design. One is tall, rustic and a little wild, while the other is low, cultured, serene—and perhaps sublime.

## The Healing Waters Fountain

The designers imagined that there would be a lengthy, rectangular reflection pool on an axis with the hospital's main entrance, reinforcing with water the hospital's architectural approach and connectivity. Rather than being formal, the fountain would be playful, immersive, fun and sparklingly delightful. The fountain would reveal different characteristics as its water presentation transformed, and it might be something like a river, suggesting time, or like a carved landscape, suggesting place, or maybe something of an even higher, spiritual quality.

A coursing, topographic channel is carved through the space of the fountain. Its cut layers form a contoured space for play. There's even a meandering path through the contours especially sloped for wheelchair access.

The fountain's different characters are generated by changing water levels and nozzle activities. In Mode 1 the waters fill the topography to overflowing, presenting a tranquil reflection surface, aligned with its surrounding walks. In this mode or any other, the water is either fairly still or actively roiling from subterranean bubbly flows, which are internally illuminated at night. Two other modes of operation establish lower reflection surface levels, and the final, fourth mode calls solemnly for an empty basin, waiting to be filled.

The articulately sculpted design is organic and non-repeating, and each of its 700-plus finished blocks is a unique shape. It is remarkable how absolutely perfectly the contours fit together, a testament to contractor craftsmanship and computer fabrication. A poetic quotation is modestly subtracted from a single row of the blocks not far from the hospital's entrance.

And the waters are lively. They glitter brilliantly in the sunlight and shine from illuminated architecture, and they make marvelous sounds. Sometimes the pool's depths are hidden beneath the garden's reflected imagery, and sometimes the water is as transparent as crystal. All day, the waters draw people in to enjoy innocent pleasures. And often enough, one sees other participants around this fountain, quietly connected but unseeing, ruminating and benefiting from its offerings.

## The Falls

An assembled, tallish row of limestone quarry outcasts is knitted together into seven subtle 'chapters', which form a kind of wall defining the north edge of the garden. Each chapter manages a stream and each stream has a different sort of path from the others. The slightest of the flows are on the ends, while the heavier flows are nearer the center. More of an 'installation' of rock, plantings and water than a fountain in any typical sense, there is a kind of story that unfolds across the chapters from one to the next.

The waters are alive. Trees are planted atop rocks and the streams and shallow pools that course through their complex layers support numerous water plantings, some flowering, others more stark. At the base is an activated reflection pool and a stone deck with a bosque of slender shade trees where popular, movable tables and chairs enjoy filtered sunlight and a sense of protection.

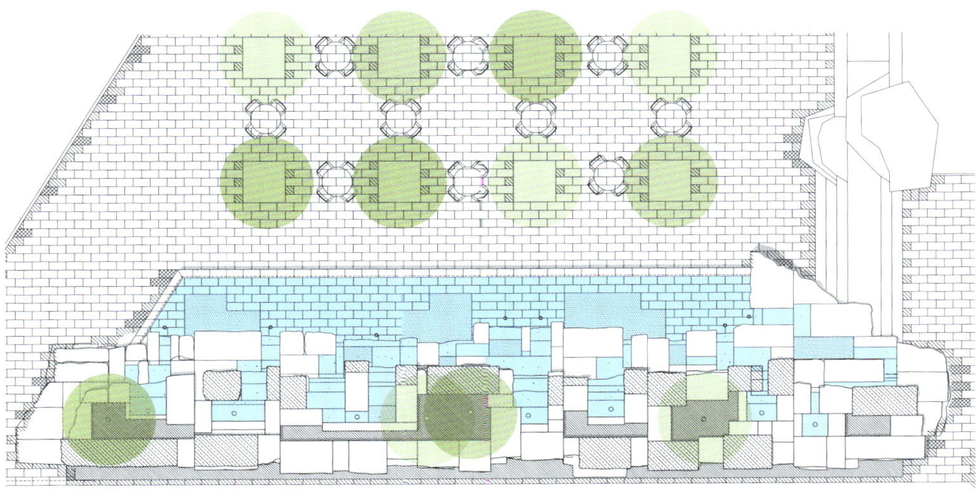

Plan of the Falls fountain, drawing by Fluidity Design Consultants

01 | Aerial view looking east over the Falls in the foreground

02 | Social life near the Falls
03 | The space of shaded tables and chairs alongside the Falls
04 | View southwest towards the Falls
05 | Water character, megalith rock wo-k, living waters plantings

West elevation

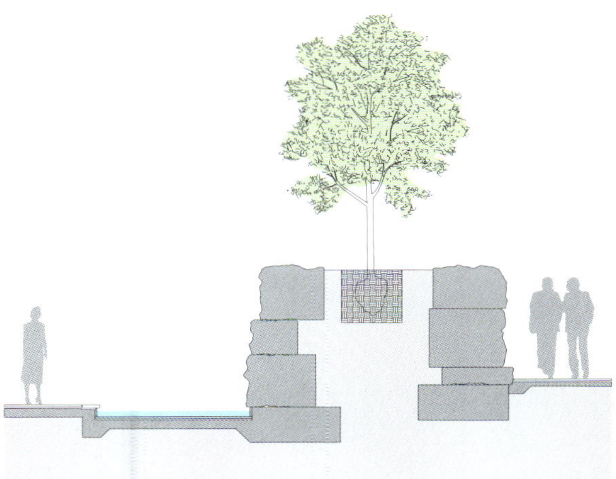

Transverse section at planter

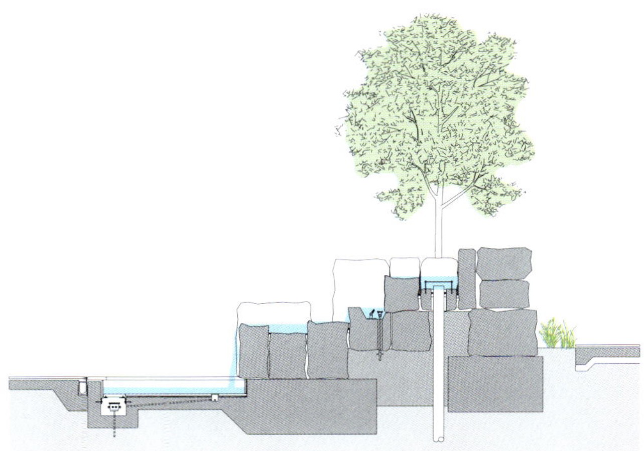

Transverse section at cascade

06

07

06 | Children at play within the Healing Waters Fountain
07–08 | Healing Waters, bubble-activated with flush-to-plaza water-level mode

Drawings by Fluidity Design Consultants

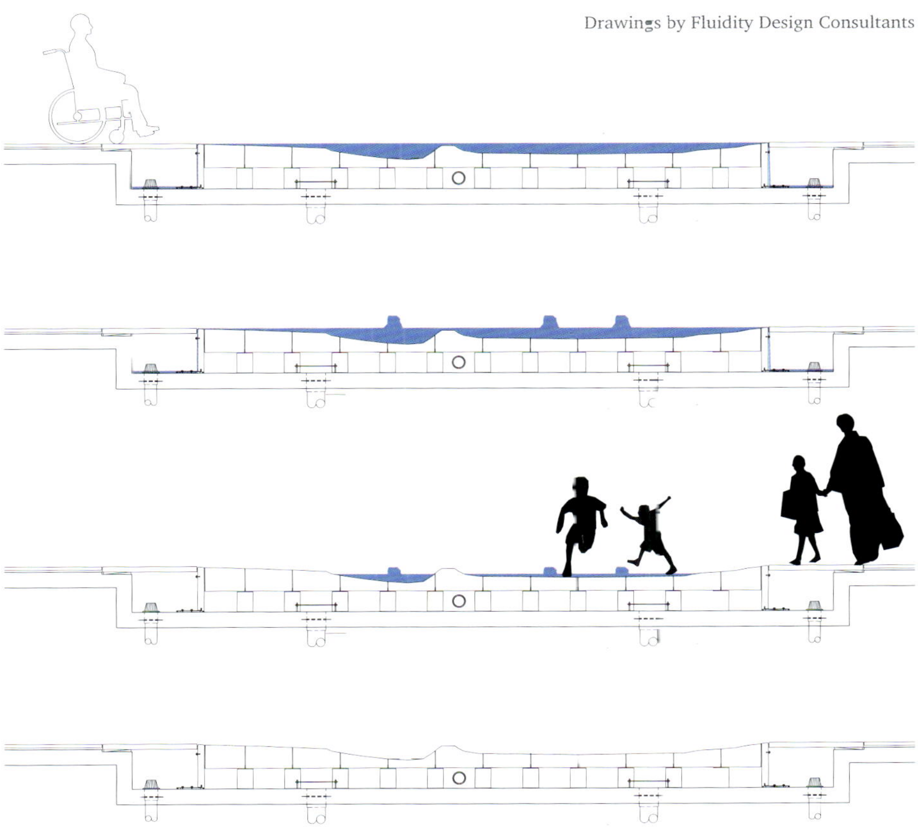

09

10

Drawings of the Healing Waters Fountain showing alternative operating water levels

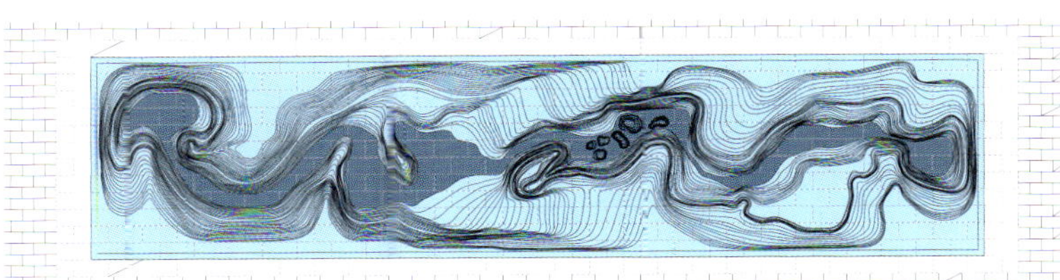

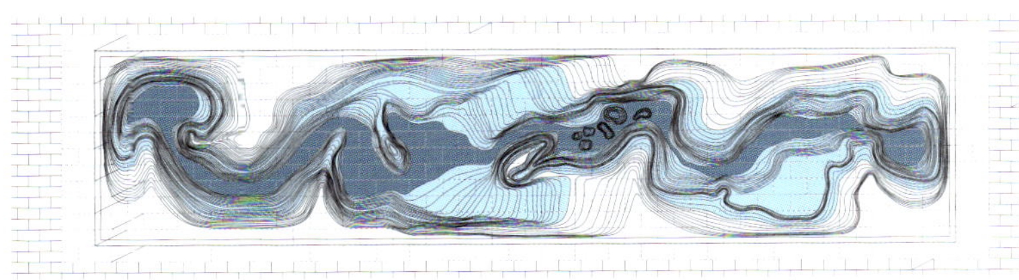

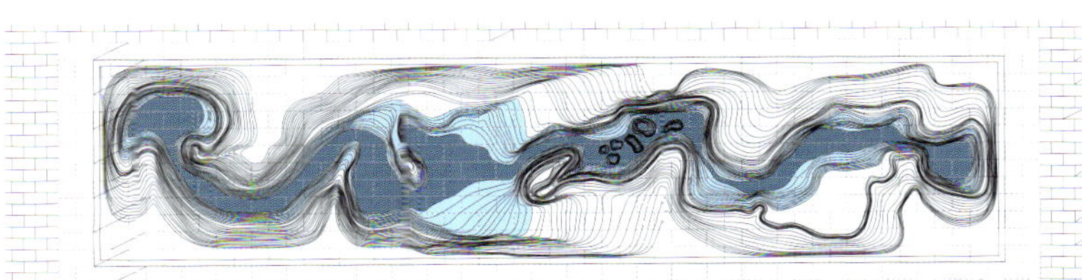

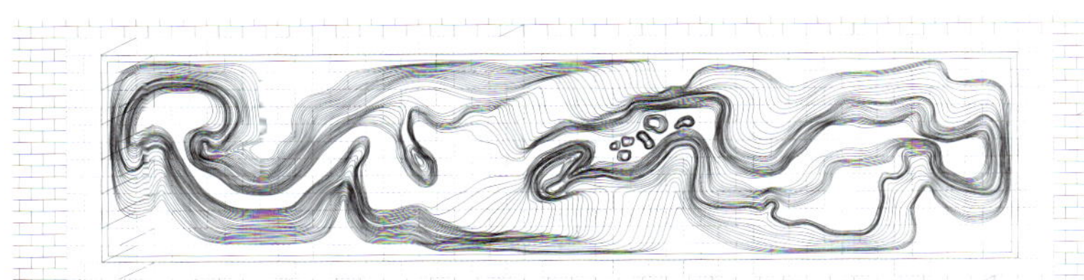

09 | Healing Waters Fountain, bubble-activated with flush-to-plaza water-level mode
10–11 | Healing Waters Fountain, bubble-activated with low water-level, topography revealed

# Zoetermeer
# Vivaldi Care Home

LOCATION
Zoetermeer, The Netherlands

AREA
7.4 acres (3 hectares)

CLIENT
Vierstroom Zorgring

COMPLETION DATE
2011

LANDSCAPE DESIGN
HOSPER

BUDGET
approx. €680,000

PHOTOGRAPHY
HOSPER

BLUEPRINT

Master plan

The care facility Vierstroom commissioned HOSPER to create a design for the public and private outdoor spaces of the Vivaldi care home in Zoetermeer. The area is surrounded by water, with flowering aquatic plants and trees on three sides. This increases the size of the area visually and, at the same time, has an important ecological function.

The building, designed by SEED Architects, has a two-sided comb structure with gardens in-between the teeth of the comb. A continuous route is possible by connecting the different gardens. The gardens either function as a scenic element or a place to visit, and are designed in such a way that there is always a good mix of green sheltered areas and more open sunny places. Wide pathways ensure that the area is well equipped to meet the needs of residents with disabilities, and creates informal places to stop and rest.

Planting was coordinated in close cooperation with gardening designer and planting advisor Jacqueline van der Kloet. The front of the building is planted with grass and large trees, thus creating a beautiful park-like atmosphere. The square at the entrance features seating furniture, bicycle stands, and a 'kiss and ride' facility. The entrance area is connected to a garden with a café/restaurant and terrace. A red pond with water plants and fish, and a series of playground elements, add to the vibrancy and appeal of this area.

At the head of the garden, in line with the central axis, lies the water garden, which consists of a higher garden on ground level; and a lower garden, accessible by ramp, which is close to the water level. A boardwalk in-between the swamp-like vegetation makes it possible for residents of all ability levels to experience the water. A fountain ensures the connection between the building, the garden and the surrounding water.

For activities such as gardening, HOSPER designed a kitchen garden/flower-picking garden with the possibility to add a greenhouse. This garden is connected to the day-care facility, the library, and the central corridor. There are flower and vegetable beds, one of which is constructed on a higher level so that it can be reached easily by residents in a wheelchair. The patio adjacent to the physical therapy room is designed as a practice garden. It's equipped with fitness equipment and different types of paving so residents can practice new physical challenges, such as walking with a walking aid.

01

02

01 | The waterfront garden
02 | Hydrangea planting in the higher water garden

07 | Overview of the water garden at the head of the care home complex
08 | Strawberries in the kitchen/flower-picking garden

09 | The kitchen/flower-picking garden

# Restorative Garden at Danbury Hospital

LOCATION
Danbury, USA

AREA
4000 square feet (371.61 square metres)

COMPLETION DATE
2012

LANDSCAPE DESIGN
Dirtworks Landscape Architecture, PC

PHOTOGRAPHY
Mark Weinberg

AWARD
2013 Landscape Architecture Awards for Healthcare Environments Bronze Winner

Danbury Hospital's Level IIIB Neonatal Intensive Care Unit (NICU) cares for newborns with the most complex medical conditions. This project, part of the hospital's NICU expansion designed by Perkins Eastman, created a 770-square-foot (71.5-square-meter) pavilion and 4000-square-foot (371.6-square-meter), second-floor rooftop garden adjacent to the NICU.

The idea for the roof garden arose during the initial planning stages for the new NICU, when the design team discovered an opportunity to locate patient rooms adjacent to a vacant roof. The garden was designed following the Planetree health-care model, which focuses on human interaction, family involvement, nurturing environments, and access to nature. Early planning focus groups involved the hospital's infection control and facilities management personnel along with patient-care staff.

A key design consideration was creating seasonally interesting views of nature from the interior rooms for families who spend weeks or months at the hospital. The challenge was to balance the desire for views with the need for privacy. The design strategically uses a green roof and deciduous and evergreen plants to provide the required buffer between indoor and outdoor views.

The garden is accessed directly from the NICU through a 'garden pavilion', which features seats and expansive views of the garden. Exiting the pavilion, a vine-covered trellis provides a seating area with dappled shade and privacy from the hospital's upper floors. The garden offers opportunities for strolling, large gathering spaces for socializing, and small intimate areas for respite and privacy. Plantings provide sensory and seasonal interest. Trees and custom wood and metal structures provide shade and privacy. These structures also screen adjacent mechanical equipment and service areas, and provide protection from winds. The overall garden organization reflects significant design and engineering coordination to address the existing roof's complex slab conditions and limited structural capacity.

BLUEPRINT

1. Pavilion
2. Passageway
3. NICU Rooms
4. Green roof
5. Wave-shaped planters
6. Planters
7. Strolling and seating areas
8. Plant displays
9. Trellis and seating areas
10. Wood and metal screen walls
11. Mechanical equipment
12. Main gathering area
13. Seat wall
14. Service corridor

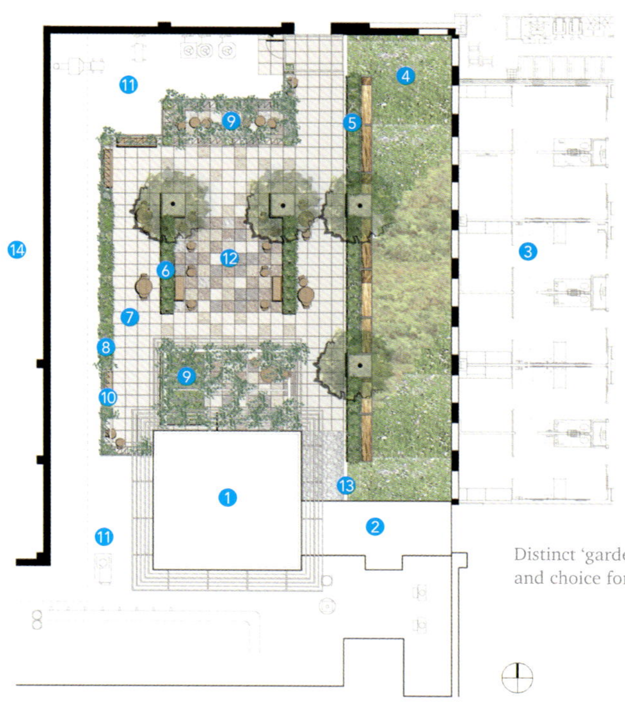

Distinct 'garden rooms' offer opportunity and choice for each visitor

01 | Views from the NICU rooms balance the desire for views with the need for privacy
02 | The garden's deceptively simple layout accommodates often-conflicting needs: solitude and socialization, respite and activity

03 | The design offers opportunities for strolling, large gathering spaces for socializing, and small intimate areas for respite and privacy

04 | A vine-covered trellis provides a seating area with dappled shade and privacy from the hospital's upper floors

05 | The Garden Pavilion provides a flexible climate-controlled space with expansive views of the garden

06

07

06 | The passageway connecting the garden and hospital offers inviting views, critical hand-washing facilities and health/safety information

07 | Visually isolated from the main spaces are intimate areas for contemplation and quiet respite

08

09

10

08 | Engaging plant displays provide seasonal interest and offer an invitation to pause
09 | Custom trellis structures create seating areas and screen mechanical equipment, while lighting ensures evening use without disturbing nearby rooms
10 | A sinuous wave-shaped planter extending the length of the garden helps screen the NICU rooms from the terrace
11 | A separate controlled entry for staff has clear views across the terrace

# Crown Sky Garden

LOCATION
Chicago, USA

CLIENT
Ann & Robert H. Lurie Children's Hospital

COMPLETION DATE
2012

LANDSCAPE DESIGN
mikyoung kim design

PHOTOGRAPHY
Hedrich Blessing, George Heinrich

AWARDS
2013 American Society of Landscape Architects (ASLA) Honor Award

Situated along the Magnificent Mile, in the heart of downtown Chicago, the Crown Sky Garden is an inspiring healing garden within a glass greenhouse on the 11th floor of the 23-story Lurie Children's Hospital. A strikingly luminous and colorful sanctuary, it provides rich sensory experiences for the young patients, families, doctors, and administrators within the hospital.

The Family Advisory Board and Lurie pediatric hospital transformed 5000 square feet (464.5 square meters) of space into a vibrant garden which demonstrates innovative thinking for child-centered health-care and healing environments. The commitment to the Sky Garden was built upon a growing body of scientific research, which links access to natural light and contemplative spaces to reduced patient recovery time. This regenerative project offers a new paradigm for health-care design that integrates healing gardens as part of the health-care regime within these institutional environments. The new pediatric center is partnering with the Center for Health Design to examine the impact of hospital design on stress levels in hospitalized children and their parents in the Crown Sky Garden.

For the patients and families, the Sky Garden offers enticing spaces of light, water, and color. The multicolored light walls frame a linear bamboo grove, while the colored glass marble fountains meander through the planters, creating dappled shade in the contemplative

BLUEPRINT

1. Outdoor balcony
2. North contemplation room
3. Terrazzo floor
4. Bamboo planter
5. Performance area/gravity wall
6. Interactive plan area light and sound
7. Bamboo planter
8. South contemplation room
9. Arts and crafts area
10. Outdoor balcony
11. Cafeteria seating area
12. To elevators

Perspective renderings

Master plan

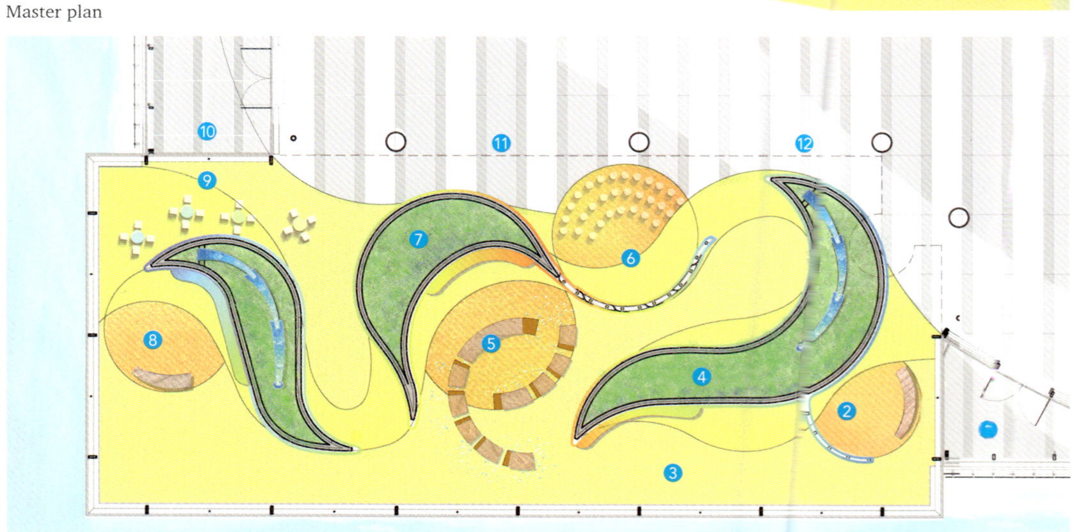

areas of the garden, which offer city views through floor-to-ceiling glass windows. There's also an opportunity in these peripheral spaces to engage with the garden at a more intimate scale. The center of the Sky Garden houses interactive elements of light and sound in the resin walls and locally reclaimed-wood play sculptures. Children activate the garden through engagement and orchestrate sounds of nature through their presence in this active space. The garden incorporates a range of individual and collective spaces that meet the needs of children with immune deficiencies, while offering a place for discovery and innovative engagement.

01 | Located on the 12th floor above the main Sky Garden and framed by the bamboo canopy from the garden below, this intimate space is designed for inpatient children with serious immune-deficiency conditions that prevent them from enjoying the the main garden

02 | This protected space has a series of longitudinal cross-sections of reclaimed wood that connect wall-to-floor surfaces and have an infill of hickory end grain panels

03 | Reclaimed-wood sculptures are located in the garden rooms and act as play elements and benches

04 | In the center of the garden, LED lights within the core of the retaining walls are choreographed to transform images of water as children activate the sensors; from calm tidal movements to intensely colorful bubbles

05 | The Light Walls are constructed with resin panels that are created with a minimum of 40 percent recycled content. The wood-log seating elements and wood flooring in the tree house are locally reclaimed materials and utilize natural non-toxic finishes

Site score: fountain sound and rhythm

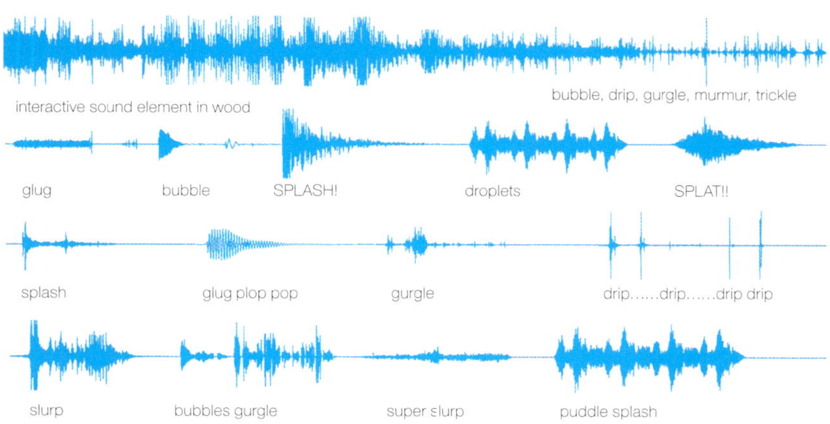


06 | Bronze hands were cast from pediatric patients in the Children's Hospital and are the sensors that activate the sounds of water that emanate from the speakers carved into the reclaimed logs

07

08

07–08 | The colored resin wall comprises a series of folded and interlocking custom eco-resin panels that transform in color from aqua to saffron colors. These gradated colored panels are an effective anti-microbial surface and create a chromatic color flow as participants move around the walls

03 | The custom granite water feature shown at dusk

04 | Visitors, patients and staff can enjoy the healing garden with the many comfortable seating options

05 | The garden canopy is constructed of steel, wood, and polycarbonate to complement the sleek, contemporary lines of the building
06 | From tables to chairs to benches and seat walls, numerous seating options are provided

# El Camino Hospital Rehabilitation Garden

LOCATION
Los Gatos, USA

AREA
7000 square feet (650.32 square meters)

CLIENT
Presbyterian Health Services

COMPLETION DATE
2013

LANDSCAPE DESIGN
INTERSTICE Architects

PHOTOGRAPHY
El Camino Hospital

BLUEPRINT

Plan

The existing site plan of the 1970 facility provided little or no landscape amenity around this 30-bed Rehabilitation Hospital. The landscape architect was hired to take a Master Plan approach to the site to identify opportunities within the existing site for significant improvements. The landscape architect identified the following Master Plan goals: 1) create connection between the interiors and the landscape through the building program, 2) create a welcoming entry experience, 3) create opportunities for therapeutic activities in a garden setting, and 4) create a sense of place and atmosphere.

Two previously neglected spaces were prioritized to create two new outdoor assets for rehabilitation: an entry garden and a therapy courtyard were to define Phase 1. A residual concrete utilities court and an abandoned ambulance drop-off area became the raw material for a transformative intervention, converting marginalized exterior spaces into usable places. The staff and facilities collaborated on the development of these two previously peripheral landscape spaces, with a strong desire to integrate therapy activities such as mobility (gait) training for patients and therapeutic gardening, in addition to family visitation.

The final design prioritized the facility's central mission: making these new places expressions of wellness and rehabilitation that extends the interior building program into the world outside the hospital, ultimately the goal and successful outcome of every patient's treatment. Emphasis was placed on developing easily negotiable spaces that brought the experience of seasonal color, fragrance, and subtle movement of grasses and butterflies into the lives of the patients to help hasten their recovery and improve their motivation.

## Entry garden

The new entry garden creates a new front door for the Inpatient Rehabilitation Center facility. The design relocated the formerly striped emergency-vehicle parking area that served as the main pedestrian entry to the facility. Staff, patients and visitors now approach through a garden setting with shade trees, pathways, and quiet seating areas for gathering and visiting with family. The under-utilized parking area was re-configured to create a vibrant and inhabitable entry garden. The organization is a simple braid of two crossing paths—one that connects two stone seating area destinations and one that travels over varying surface paving and up over a graduated sequence of steps and ramps meant for re-learning mobility.

## Therapy courtyard

Given the challenges of size limitations and the residual geometries resulting from the existing buildings, a perimeter infrastructure of built-in planters, vine screens, trellises and wooly pockets were used to create green surfaces, which also define and unify the landscape spaces. The lighting design strategy uses a plane of festoon-type overhead lights and kick-mounted LED lights to extend the use of the therapy courtyard, connect it visually to the gym, and unify it spatially. Plants were selected carefully both for seasonal change and attraction of butterflies and bird-life. Annual vegetable plantings were included to offer opportunities for gardening therapy, both for sitting and standing patients. The formerly unused landscape is now an integral part of the therapy regimes used to treat rehabilitating patients.

01 | The Hospital Rehabilitation Garden is accessible for all the patients, including wheelchair users
02 | Seating area at dusk
03 | Seating area and planters

04–06 | Green wall in seating area

07–09 | Annual vegetable plantings were included to offer opportunities for gardening therapy, both for sitting and standing patients

# Kaiser Permanente San Leandro Medical Center

LOCATION
San Leandro, California, USA

CLIENT
Kaiser Permanente

COMPLETION DATE
2014

LANDSCAPE DESIGN
AECOM

PHOTOGRAPHY
Terence Lee

This project transformed a former industrial site in the suburban neighborhoods of San Leandro into a new regional health-care facility. As a brownfield site, much of its site concrete was demolished and reused for site aggregate material as part of the project's sustainable development approach. During the early project-planning phase, retail and residential use were designated to be adjacent to the north edge of the project site. Therefore, it was imperative to plan for pedestrian linkages and appropriate adjacent land use, while providing a welcoming entry to the main hospital building.

The site areas immediately surrounding the hospital were treated as a welcoming public plaza capable of hosting a variety of uses. From farmers' markets to event fairs, ample open plaza space was planned for temporary tents and outdoor access to power and other utilities. Carefully planned seat walls and landscape berms allow enclosure while remaining open and flexible. To the east of the building, an intricate stone plaza designed in the pattern of a labyrinth offered further seating and a peaceful respite. Located within the patient rooms portion of the building is an intimate courtyard filled with bamboo planters and meandering paths that allow multiple seating and gathering opportunities. The courtyard also offered a spill-out dining plaza adjacent to the interior cafeteria.

Beyond the immediate surroundings of the building is an extensively planted and sustainably designed surface parking lot employing substantial bio-swales to control rainwater runoff. The adapted plant palette is also arranged in a unique pattern of identifiable plants and tree types in specific areas of the parking lot. The sense of nature is also referenced on a conceptual level by shaping the planted berms in the shape of fallen leaves, while the plaza paving is interrupted by irregularly shaped bars of colored paving resembling branches and twigs.

To promote health and well-being, the site features a 1-mile (1.5-kilometer) jogging path with multiple exercise stations. The layout of the site and parking lots were also designed for future facility expansion, capable of adding without significantly damaging the rest of the site. Possible new developments include two medical office buildings, two parking structures as well as an additional clinical wing, and emergency department expansion for the hospital.

BLUEPRINT

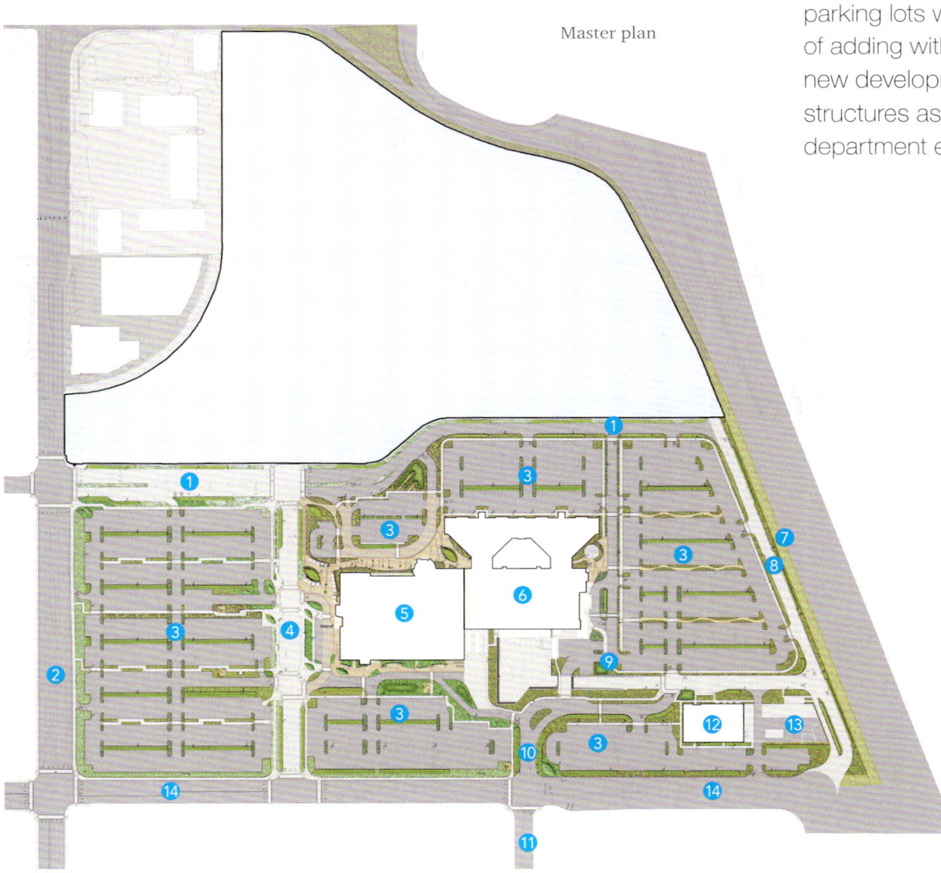

Master plan

① Entry drive/Republic Avenue extension
② Merced street
③ Parking
④ West Medical Center driveway
⑤ Hospital support building
⑥ Hospital
⑦ Freeway
⑧ Frontage road
⑨ Ambulance yard
⑩ South entry
⑪ Miller Street
⑫ Central utility plant
⑬ Service yard
⑭ Fairway drive

Planting zones

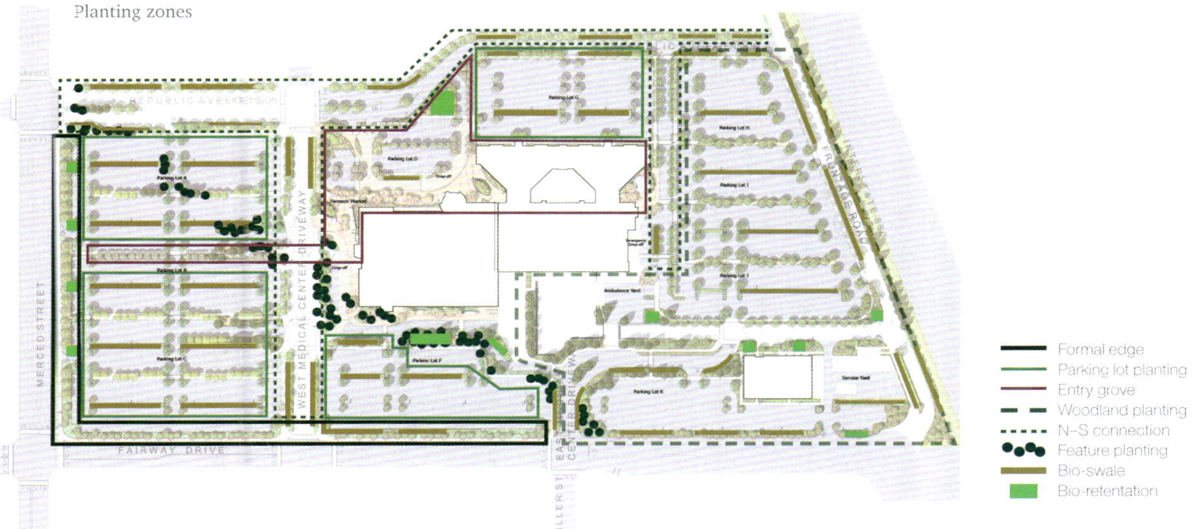


01 | Meandering paths in the bamboo courtyard
02 | Cafeteria tables and chairs spill out onto the courtyard

03

04

05

03 | Welcoming entry landscape with uninterrupted view of the building entrance
04 | Unique paving patterns and shade-friendly plants greet the visitor at the patient drop-off zone
05 | Leaf-shaped planted mounds bordered by seat walls for sitting opportunity for patient, family or staff

Detailed planting plan

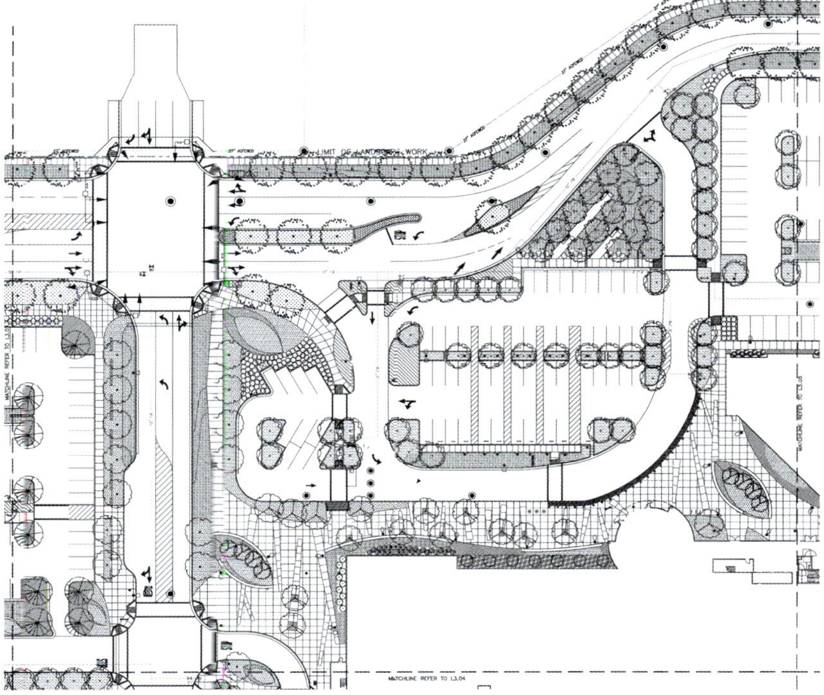

06 | Peaceful labyrinth for respite and contemplation

07 | Compacted decomposed-granite paths with native grasses meander through east parking lot

# Joel Schnaper Memorial Garden

Since 1995, the Joel Schnaper Memorial Garden in the Terence Cardinal Cooke Health Care Center has provided an oasis of peace and tranquillity for residents and visitors alike. The garden also serves as a convenient location for social activities, ranging from parties to exercise classes to small gatherings. In 2004, building upgrades necessitated that the garden be totally removed. Dirtworks, PC was asked to rebuild the garden to continue the health-care center's vision and mission of care, and to extend the life of the garden for decades of enjoyment.

Designed pro bono by David Kamp, FASLA, LF and founding principal of Dirtworks, PC, this important work is a reflection of the firm's design philosophy—to provide opportunity for everyone to connect with nature on their own terms, in their own way and at their own pace, regardless of their capabilities.

Located in the East Harlem community across from Central Park, the Terence Cardinal Cooke Health Care Center is a long-term care facility serving more than 700 residents. It provides services to the elderly and people with a range of developmental disabilities and chronic illnesses, including residents with HIV. The rooftop garden welcomes all residents visitors and staff while providing a therapeutic environment for the adjacent AIDS care wing. The garden, built totally with donations and volunteer labor, is dedicated to Joel Schnaper, a landscape architect who specialized in urban gardens, and sadly died of AIDS.

The Joel Schnaper Memorial Garden is a restorative garden; it shows the effectiveness of gardens to influence and enhance the quality of the health-care environment. It advances the idea that properly planned and operated gardens can reduce stress and encourage a sense of well-being for long-term health-care patients.

LOCATION
New York, USA

AREA
8400 square feet (780.39 square meters)

CLIENT
Terence Cardinal Cooke Health Care Center

COMPLETION DATE
2004

LANDSCAPE DESIGN
Dirtworks Landscape Architecture, PC

PHOTOGRAPHY
Randall Schieber, Nick Fancher

BLUEPRINT

1. Entry
2. Entry vestibule
3. View from patient room
4. Seasonal central display
5. Promendade
6. Demonstration farm
7. Activity pavilion
8. Activity pavilion with fabric canopy
9. Service/storage area
10. Vine-covered pavilion
11. View from lounge

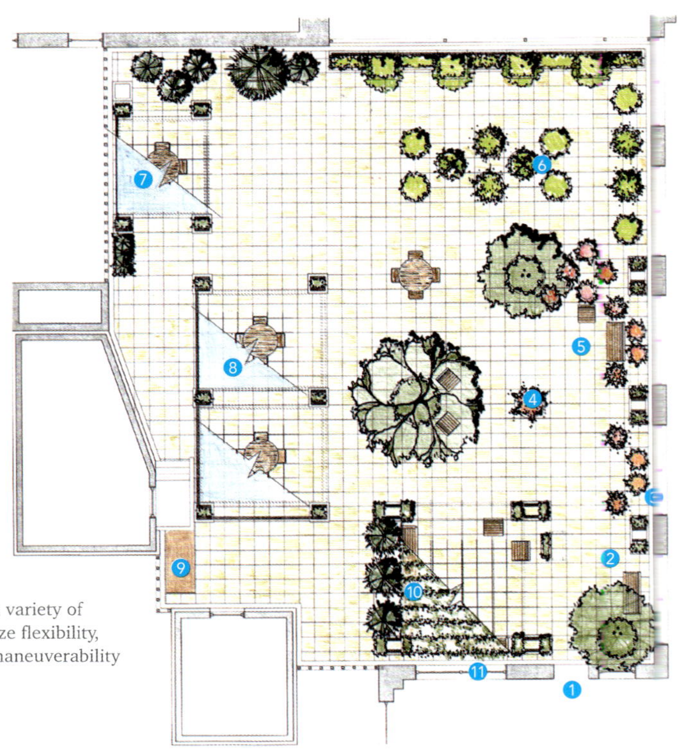

The design creates a variety of spaces that emphasize flexibility, clarity and ease of maneuverability

The garden's design focuses on the specific needs and requirements of the HIV resident. Numerous concerns are addressed, such as strength and stamina, varying sensory abilities, sunlight sensitivity, awareness, orientation and the need for activity, interaction, privacy, and independence. Plant selections play a vital role in providing a sense of empowerment through careful use of color, fragrance, texture, sound, and taste. Plants also link the garden with the center's physical and occupational therapy programs by advancing the therapeutic value of nature as a complement to traditional medical and social programs.

The garden offers a variety of spaces that are flexible in size and arrangement with varying degrees of enclosure and privacy. The garden can accommodate large events while also providing intimate settings for private activities or quiet moments. Fully accessible to the physically challenged, the layout emphasizes clarity and ease of maneuverability to encourage individuals to experience the garden without assistance.

The garden provides a hierarchy of protective settings depending upon personal comfort and medication protocols, varying from complete shade under tent structures, to dappled sun/shade under vines and tree canopies to open areas with full sunlight.

Planters vary in size and height for individual ease of use. Circular planters create mini-gardens that provide enjoyment for visitors and residents. Easy access to these mini-gardens encourages individual and group activities, casual conversation, and instruction.

Design is a reflection of the qualities of our lives, expressing our hopes and aspirations in how we choose to live and to heal. Through restorative gardens, nature and design join together, broadening our understanding of how compassionate care and the natural environment can enrich healing and strengthen the human spirit.

01 | The Demonstration Farm is the center of horticultural and recreational therapy

02 | The garden accommodates large events as well as small group activities and private respite
03 | Accommodating individual health needs and levels of comfort, the garden provides a progression of protective settings

04 Viewed from the entry, the garden creates a sense of welcome by offering a rich sensory experience, whatever the individual's capacity

05 | Easily arranged tables and chairs can be found throughout the garden for private moments and program activities

06 | With clear views across the garden, staff can relax while keeping an eye on groups and activities

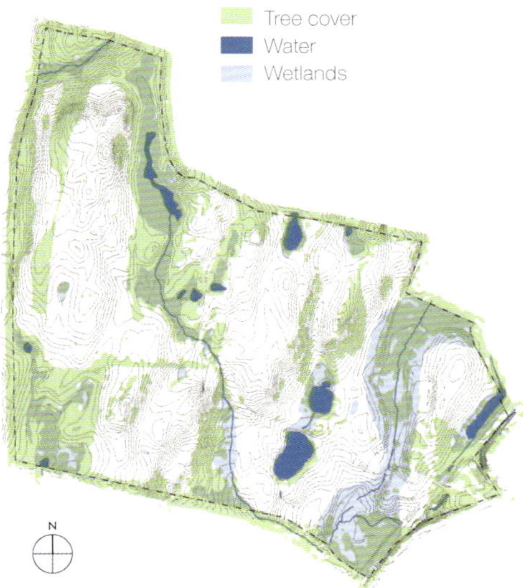


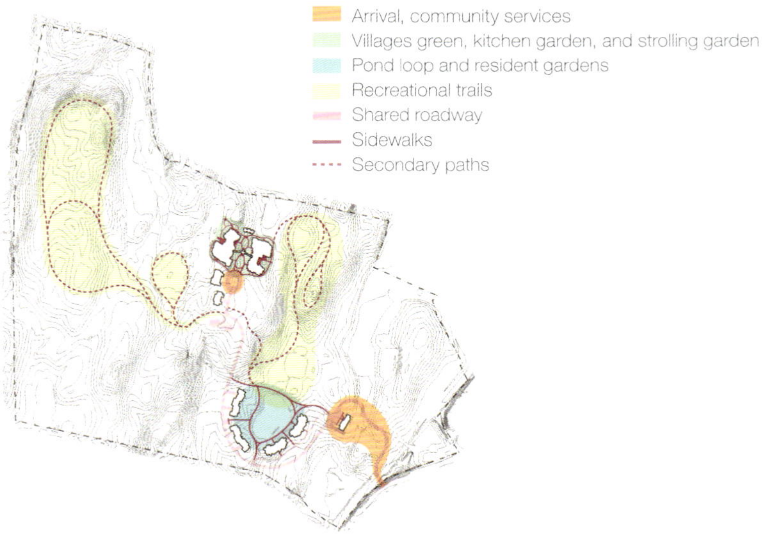


The site was planned to enhance wildlife corridors and preserve the natural watershed and hydrological network

04

05

03 | A network of gently graded sidewalks connects neighboring buildings
04 | An existing barn was reconstructed in the region's vernacular architectural style to serve as a community center
05 | A network of more challenging trails extend across the site for more active recreation and exploration

06 | Wetlands and the natural hydrology of the site were preserved and enhanced
07 | The path system encourages exercise and creates a sense of immersion within the natural environment
08 | Porches and patios provide immediate and comfortable access to the outdoors
09 | A variety of outdoor spaces are provided, including a village green, strolling gardens, and kitchen gardens

07

08

09

Dining courtyard

Chapel courtyard

02 | Sitting area at the end of the dining courtyard
03 | Colored glass blocks glow in the high desert sun
04 | Accessible seating is tucked into garden spaces
05 | Perspective study, chapel courtyard
06 | Native plants connect visitors to their regional landscapes
07 | Art is arranged throughout the garden landscapes

① Hosta big blue
② Dedication plaque
③ Dedication bollard
④ Dedication bench
⑤ Pale purple Echinacea
⑥ Ivory silk lilac
⑦ Tabletop juniper
⑧ Pennisetum Hameln
⑨ Dense yew
⑩ Periwincle groundcover
⑪ Existing tree
⑫ Gold ninebark
⑬ Sedum 'autumn joy'
⑭ Blue false cypress
⑮ Amur maple
⑯ Rudbeckia
⑰ Panicum 'heavy metal' in river

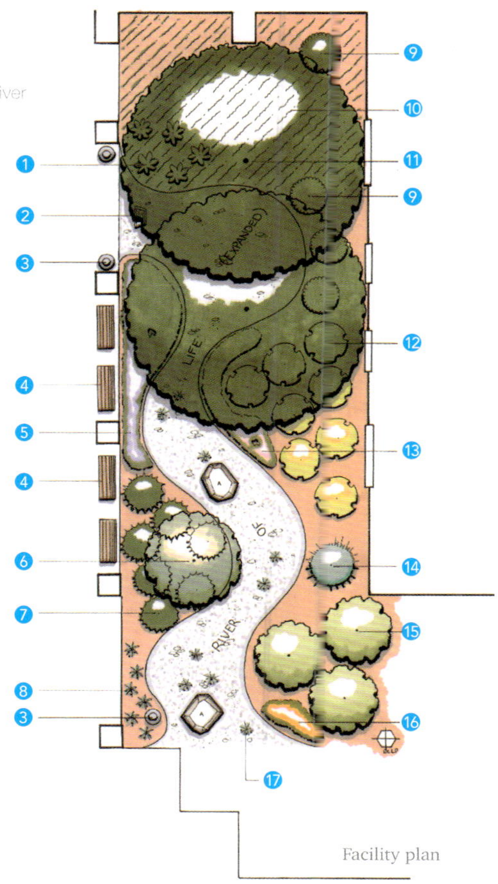

Facility plan

02 | Panoramic view of the Garden of Fond Memories
03–04 | Memorial bench and entryway bridge

05 | Interior courtyard stone seating area
06 | Close up of River of Life with engraved memorial stone

03 | An ornamental metal fence with granite base secures the courtyard's public entrance
04 | Colorful tables and umbrellas offer comfortable seating for all who use the courtyard
05 | The courtyard is composed of concrete, concrete paver insets, and granite highlights

06

07

08

09

06 | Mail and newspaper delivery boxes provide real-life situations to aid strength and agility therapy
07 | A series of gates and latching mechanisms provide exercise and dexterity therapy
08 | Sustainable hardwood highlights a planting trellis, bench with backrest, and ball court backstop against grey tone pavements
09 | A New England–style pergola provides an elegant shaped structure
10 | An adjustable basketball hoop is set into a sports surface; a retractable side mesh keeps the balls inside the court while in use

Concept sketch plan

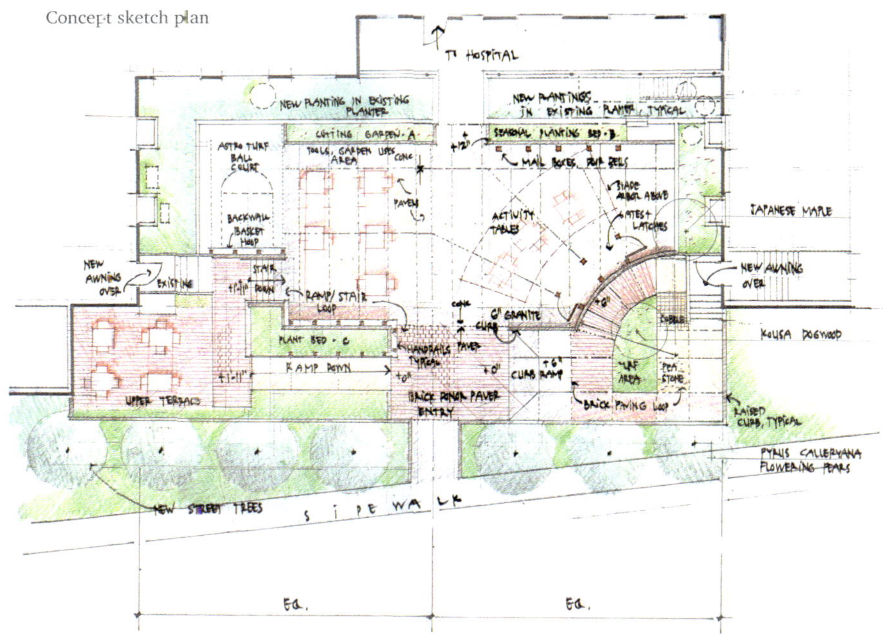

# Valencia Old Hospital Gardens Rehabilitation Project

LOCATION
Valencia, Spain

AREA
6.5 acres (2.6 hectares)

CLIENT
Diputación de Valencia (1st phase)
Conselleria d'obres Publiques, Urbanisme i Transports-Generalitat Valenciana (2nd phase)

COMPLETION DATE
2013

LANDSCAPE DESIGN
Guillermo Vázquez Consuegra

BUDGET
€4,857,131

PHOTOGRAPHY
David Frutos, David Zarzoso, Alfonso Legaz, Estudio Vazquez Consuegra

The project for the rehabilitation of the existing gardens of Valencia's Old Hospital is based on the central idea of giving a unified treatment to the entire garden area. The location was once the site of the 15th-century Hospital de los Pobres Inocentes, an important example of an historic Spanish hospital complex. In 1974, the hospital was demolished, with only the transept of the old nursing complex, the Capitulet and the little Chapel of Santa Lucia surviving the demolition. The gardens were earmarked for renovation due to the general deterioration of the conditions in the park and the construction of the nearby Museum of Illustration. It was envisaged that the renovation and reorganization of the whole garden would highlight the former role of the open spaces as the site of the old hospital building, and emphasize that the existing buildings are only fragments of the demolished hospital complex.

The existing gardens are located at a slightly elevated level of the street, which corresponds to the first line of stone blocks of the hospital that was not removed. Before the renovation, the green space was characterized by a variety of different trees and archaeological remains scattered everywhere. A system of earthen paths, with staggered geometry, defined the different areas.

The landscape architects proposed flooring in only one material, to be organized on a grid. A 'tapestry' of small pieces of basalt was laid out based on Cartesian geometry, taking its axis from the main piece of the gardens—the transept of the old nursing complex, now converted into the public library.

Over this carpet of basalt, sunken areas appear. One of them, without vegetation, has become an orchard of orange trees, a safe area with accommodation for all the archaeological remains, once scattered throughout the landscaped area. The project also involved other archaeological interventions—especially the ancient church of the hospital, which is bigger than the neighboring church of Santa Lucia. The proposal included the excavation of its archaeological remains to the depth suggested by its foundation, and the reorganization of the interior space as an area of gardens—sunken and shady spaces, protected from heavy traffic in the area, under the big crowns of the trees.

BLUEPRINT

Existing trees

New tree planting

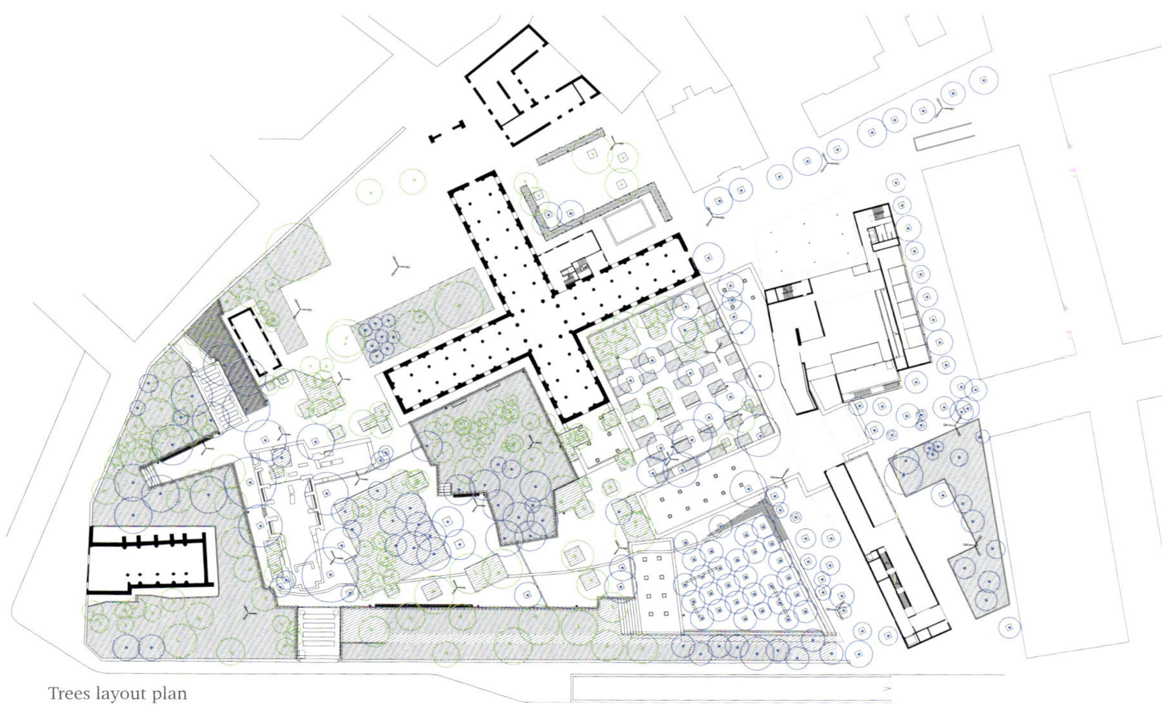

Trees layout plan

The proposal maintains the actual level of the garden so that access is available through existing doorways, now covered by steel-frame pergolas that help lead visitors to the interior of the garden. Two new entrances were created: one from Museum of the Enlightenment next to the new Museum of Illustration, demolishing small residual spaces and walls; and another, the most important, from the street hospital. It provides access to the gardens as well as the library.

A soft, wide ramp connects the level of flooring and the garden indoors. The intact columns from the old hospital rooms have been placed over this ramp, creating a new outdoor hall with 24 columns. The visitor enters the garden through this sloping room, where a grid of stone columns formalize this new lobby, thus diverting the actual access through the old Gothic doorway of the hospital.

Other diverse spaces have been established, including green outdoor rooms, children's playgrounds, metal skins covered with climbing plants for the irrelevant lateral façades of the Capitulet, and a garden enclosed by ponds and brightly colored flowers.

01

02

03

01 | Entrance pavilion to the gardens with the archeological remains, dating from the demolition of the Faculty of Medicine
02 | The façade of the Faculty of Medicine, in which the main entrance with its reliefs and the figure of Asclepius stand out
03 | Previous state—the entrance reliefs in the garden before the intervention

04 | The main entrance to the pavilion, enclosed with the three reliefs
05 | A steel pergola structurally interlocks the three reliefs and covers the new transit space
06 | The Asclepius sculpture now dominates the new pavilion
07 | The archeological remains interlock with the new steel structure, creating a new entity

07

Pergola details

Section

17

18

19

17–20 | The archeological remains of less importance, which could not be placed in their original sites, are exhibited on horizontal shelves in the orange grove's sunken area, protected from the heavy traffic on Gillem de Castro street

20

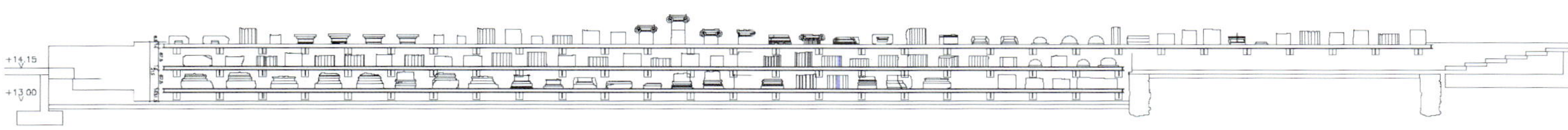

Orange trees plaza section

# Hospice Djursland

LOCATION
Djursland, Denmark

AREA
0.47 acres and 968.75-square-foot extension (1900 square metres and 90-square-meter extension)

CLIENT
Den Selvejende Institution Ejendommen Hospice Djursland

COMPLETION DATE
2011

LANDSCAPE DESIGN
C.F. Møller Architects

BUDGET
DKK 40 million

PHOTOGRAPHY
Adam Moerk

AWARDS
2012 British Civic Trust Award

BLUEPRINT

Located in a beautiful setting overlooking the bay of Aarhus, the Hospice Djursland is a palliative treatment facility with room for 15 patients. During the design process, the landscape team of C.F. Møller Architects aimed to create surroundings that would provide the best possible conditions to promote quality of life, respect, and a dignified death. They aimed to create a very humane building—a building that is not an institution, but rather a home, with adequate physical and mental space for patients in the later stages of their lives, as well as for their relatives and the staff.

Hospice Djursland is first and foremost a building within a landscape. No matter where you go in the building—the reception area, the garden of the senses, the atriums, the staff room, the lounge, the reflection room, or the patient rooms—the beautiful landscape is always present. The semi-circular layout ensures that all patient rooms enjoy an equally privileged view over the bay, and that they are located within a more private zone in the building, set back from the common rooms. Each room has a private terrace overlooking the landscape, and a section of the roof draws daylight deep into the rooms, providing a skylight over the sleeping area and the bathroom, and a soft curve to the ceiling.

The common materials used throughout are copper, oak, and glass, which interact beautifully and naturally with the landscape and provide a sense of warmth in the rooms. The landscape and gardens surrounding the hospice have been designed with special emphasis on the sensory aspects of sight, smell, touch, and sound, as well as a focus on overall accessibility for patients, even those confined to beds. The result is a series of soft, rounded shapes and niches joined by green rubber–bitumen surfaces. A new orangery winter garden has been added as an extension of the hospice. Filled with exotic plants, such as an olive tree, vine, laurel and Japanese bamboo, the winter garden makes it possible to enjoy the pleasures of outdoor life all year round. Like the rest of the hospice and the sensory garden, the orangery is easily accessible for both wheelchair users and bedridden patients.

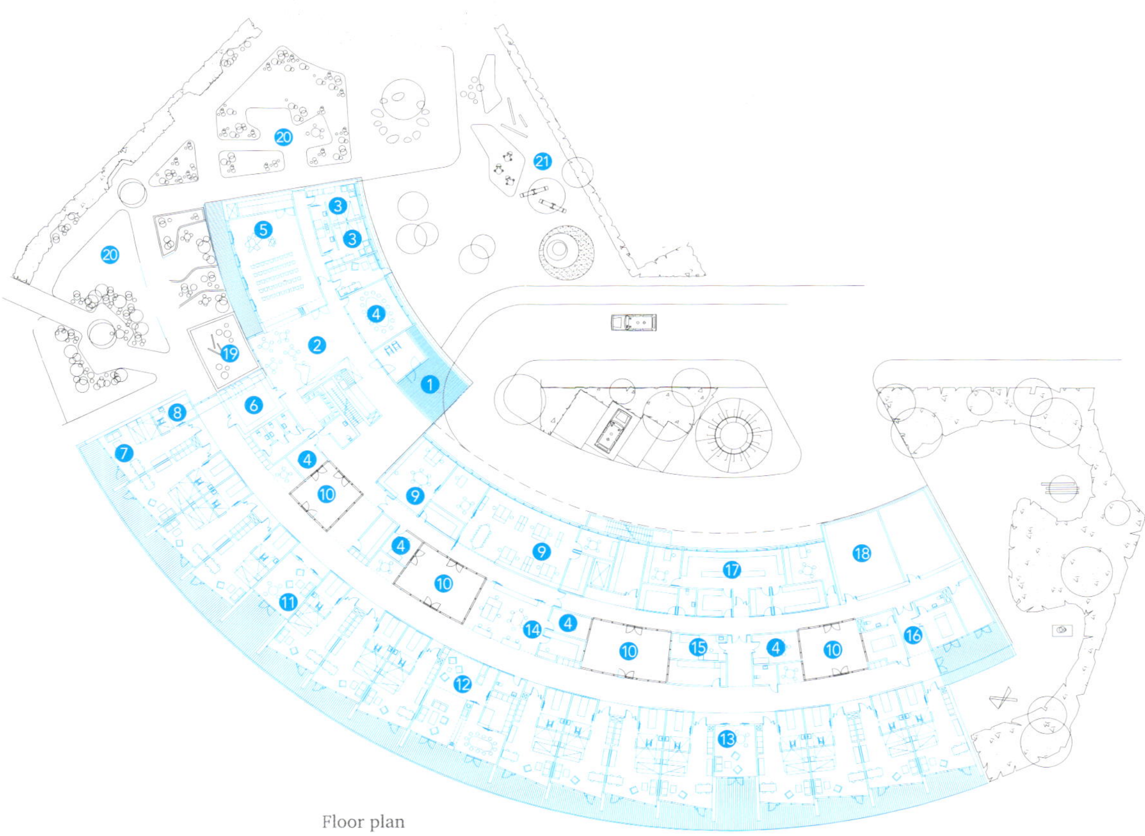

Floor plan

1. Entrance
2. Foyer/café
3. Guest accommodation
4. Meeting
5. Assembly hall
6. Meditation
7. Accommodation
8. Bathroom
9. Administration/offices
10. Courtyard gardens
11. Music room
12. Lounge/fireplace
13. Library
14. Public lounge/play area
15. Treatment rooms
16. Spa rooms
17. Kitchen
18. Garage/workshop
19. Reflecting pool
20. Sensory gardens
21. Playground

01 | The curvature of the building gives all rooms an equal share of the beautiful landscape setting
02 | The sensory gardens feature flowering and fragrant plants that stimulate the senses and evoke memories

03 | The hospice is set in a beautiful location overlooking the bay of Aarhus
04 | The patient rooms are orientated toward the views of the bay, while the common rooms overlook the garden
05 | The design is taking advantage of the setting by making the landscape ever-present inside the building
06 | Local tree turns into blossom

Sketch

07

Sketch

08

09

10

07 | The sensory gardens have been designed for maximum accessibility for all patients
08 | The soft, rounded shapes of the gardens and the green rubber–bitumen surfaces accommodate wheelchair users and bedridden patients
09 | These plants are accessible for patients who want to feel and touch nature
10 | A small pond mirrors light into the skylit reflection room inside the hospice, which is used for meditation and ceremonies

11

12

Sketch

11 | The choice of untreated oak and copper cladding gives the building a dignified expression that ages gracefully
12 | Interior and exterior are designed to blend in the covered garden spaces
13 | Every patient room enjoys a private covered terrace

14 | The orangery/conservatory adds covered outdoor garden spaces and secluded terraces
15 | Patient enjoy wonderful sunshine
16 | The orangery/conservatory during the day

17 | Interior courtyards bring light and greenery deep into the building

04 | The bamboo groves create a sense of privacy and intimacy
05 | Built-in benches with planters filled with Raphis palms provide for a moment's rest and a view to the outdoors from the south-facing windows
06 | The bamboo groves also provide a refreshing view from the waiting areas, the welcome desk and consultation rooms

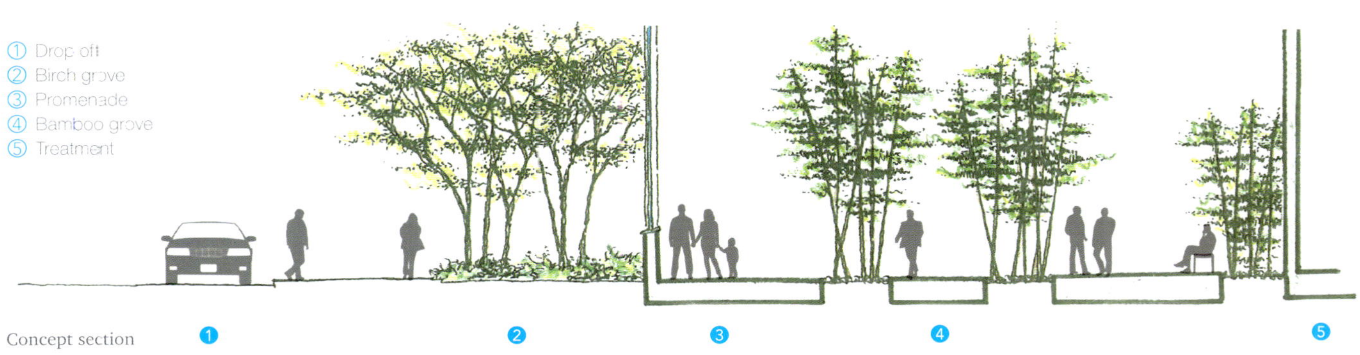


Concept section

01 | The hospital garden looks like an oasis in the desert
02 | Local drought-tolerant plants

# Veterans Affairs

LOCATION
Mojave, USA

AREA
120 acres (48.56 hectares)

LANDSCAPE DESIGN
RTKL

PHOTOGRAPHY
RTKL/David Whitcomb

Positioned on 120 acres (48.56 hectares) of open land in the northeastern portion of the Mojave Desert, a region influenced by the Sonoran Desert to the southeast and the Great Basin Desert to the north, the Department of Veterans Affairs' new medical center includes an inpatient hospital and ambulatory care center, nursing home, and infrastructure facilities. Set within the Creosote Bursage Flats of the Lower Sonoran Life Zone, the new medical center rests within a vast expanse of seemingly uniform height shrubs on desert flatlands.

Developed in response to the modern era of patient care and customer service, this new 21-acre (8.6-hectare) medical campus supports the growing client base in the American southwest. The new facility consolidates hospital-based services from multiple small sites across the region, streamlining and easing access to primary, secondary, and tertiary clinical services.

The landscape and site concept for the medical campus draws

07

08

09

06–08 | Courtyard with seating area for patients to relax
09 | Garden view from indoors

# Tokyo Metropolitan Geriatric Hospital Garden

LOCATION
Tokyo, Japan

AREA
204,514 square feet (19,000 square meters)

CLIENT
Tokyo Metropolitan Geriatric Hospital and Institute Of Gerontology

COMPLETION DATE
2013

LANDSCAPE DESIGN
Yoshiki Toda Landscape & Architect Co., Ltd.

PHOTOGRAPHY
Yoshiki Toda Landscape & Architect Co., Ltd.

Tokyo Metropolitan Geriatric Hospital Garden, part of Tokyo Metropolitan Geriatric Hospital and Institute Of Gerontology, extended the hospital's aim of promoting senior citizens' health and longevity. The purpose of building this garden is to provide a healing place for patients as well as local residents and visitors to relax.

There were two important planning objectives: one was to preserve the existing historical scenery and provide a secure and comfortable environment, the other was to service the patients, who are mainly senior citizens and local residents. The design team protected and kept the existing mature trees on the field, so that original and familiar scenery was kept. In the mean time, they introduced new plants, so users could accept the transformed garden easily. Considering that most of the users are senior citizens and patients, to make this garden more accessible, all the facilities are barrier-free, so even wheelchair users can enjoy this garden without assistance.

To create a familiar environment, some tall tree species such as Zelkovas, Prunus, and Platanus were transplanted, in order to create a sense of the secure and familiar about the place, especially those old trees that remind people of the original appearance of the place. The shade of these mature trees eases the torment of mobility-impaired users in summer. Beaches under the tall trees become perfect reading places for patients on sunny days. The familiar and popular cherry tree adds familiarity. Local aromatic plants throw off pleasing smells which attracts patients' attention in some degree, helping them forget their illness for a short time. Sculptures on the green belt were designed and placed carefully by artist. When users look at the cute sculptures, these sculptures often remind them of the happy times of their youth.

BLUEPRINT

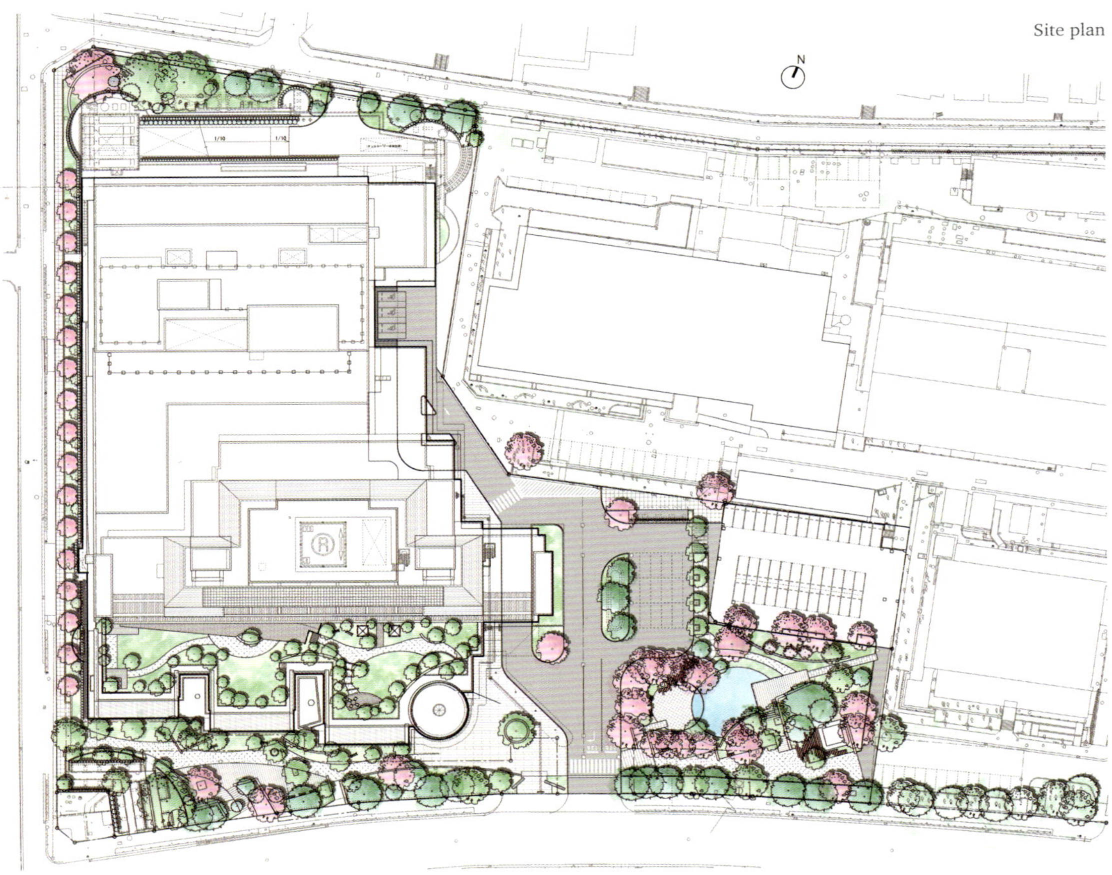


Site plan

This healing garden provides a colorful and relaxed environment; the green corridor under the tall trees provides patients with a place to walk around and breath fresh air; the waterfront space provides a resting square, stone furniture and sculptures; the cherry tree line was restored at the west side of the property facing the train line. On the north side of the property, among transplanted Prunus and Zelkovas, indigenous young trees were planted to realize the 'restoration of the forest'. The built garden plays an active part on patients' healing. The design concept of Tokyo Metropolitan Geriatric Hospital garden complies with users' practical needs, which is also a directive of healthcare landscape design.

This healing garden is supposed to be a public therapeutic garden, which provides a comfortable and quiet environment for not only patients but also for the surrounding community by creating more vital and liveable landscapes.

01–02 | Plants in the healing garden during springtime

03–04 | Local stone gabions
05 | The existing trees provide comfort with their familiarity

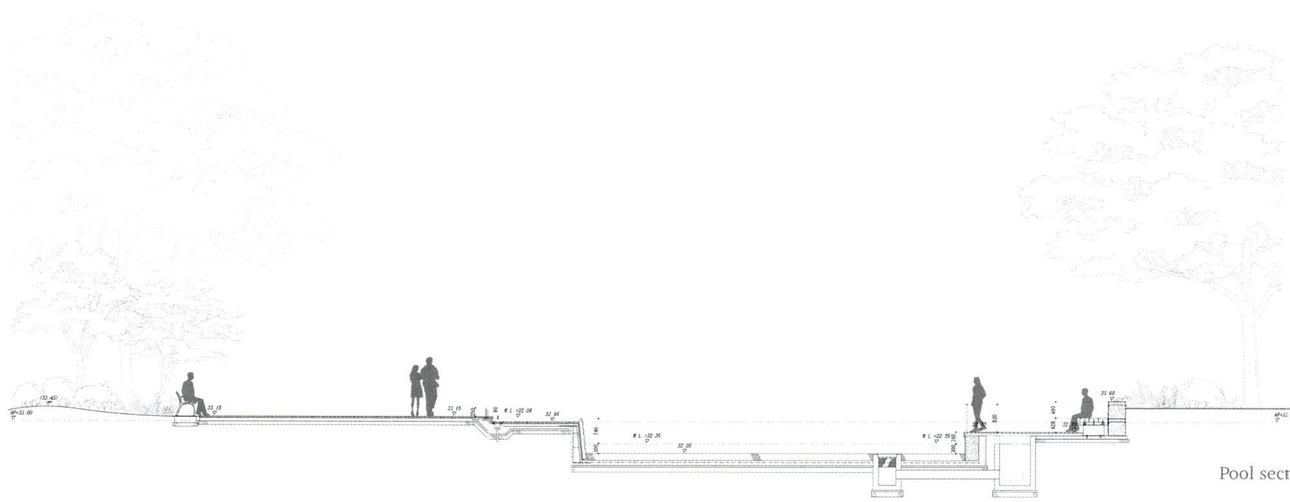

Pool section

Garden section

# Sculpture Garden

LOCATION
Ramat Gan, Israel

AREA
53,820 square feet (5000 square metres)

CLIENT
Sheba Academic Medical Center Hospital

COMPLETION DATE
2006

LANDSCAPE DESIGN
Haussmann Architects Ltd.

BUDGET
US$600,000

PHOTOGRAPHY
Assaf Pinchuk, Elisha Haussmann

BLUEPRINT

Master plan

The Sculpture Garden, located in the Sheba Medical Center, is an example of a growing trend in which hospitals around the world strive to broaden the term 'treatment' and enhance their efficiency with the use of a multi-disciplinary approach. The Sheba Medical Center was established in 1948 in the center of Israel, and is one of the largest, most advanced medical centers in the country today. Over the years, the rehabilitation center has developed a holistic philosophical approach that uses a diversity of tools to accomplish the goal of healing. The facilities of the rehabilitation hospital, the 'Lev' Medical Hotel, and many parks and gardens sit side by side, providing a complementary system on the road to full recovery.

The Sculpture Garden is part of a larger walking track, the 2.2-mile (3.5-kilometer) Trail of Health, a relaxing pathway through parks and gardens that surrounds the medical center, and was designed for the benefit of patients, medical staff, and the center's guests. The northern part of the Trail of Health meets the southern entrance of the Sculpture Garden, creating a continuous flow and connecting the pathway with its surroundings.

The structure of the garden was designed to be accessible and provide physical and mental support to the patients of the rehabilitation center. The garden has been specially designed for the needs of patients who have suffered from heart attacks.

The experience of strolling in the garden is the primary consideration in its design, influencing the planning stage to a great extent. There are two main paths within the garden. The first is a centered, straight path that crosses from one side to the other, with sculptures located along its length. The second is a curved path that runs throughout the garden, with loops around the sculptures, offering visitors many viewpoints to the sculptures and the garden. The path creates division for the inner spaces, and a sense of concealment and reveal throughout the garden. Trees, lawns, and sitting areas along the curved path provide intimate, shady places for people to relax and explore the sculptures that surround them.

The Sculpture Garden is a healing, holistic, and interactive place, with carefully chosen plantings to create a relaxing, low-stress atmosphere. The still elements in the garden—such as trails, sitting walls, benches, and sculptures—encourage visitors to interact and connect with their surroundings, creating an uplifting, stimulating experience.

Various artists donated the sculptures that feature in the garden. The trails were designed to allow people to move comfortably through the space, so asphalt and textured concrete were chosen for ease of movement. The curved trail has a steady, mild slope and a low sitting wall edging the path. It features a granolith finish and ipe wooden seats to provide additional rest stops. The planted areas combine with the walking paths to create a colorful, calming picture to the eye and soul.

The garden is an integral part of the medical treatment in the Sheba Medical Rehabilitation Center. Prescriptions given by doctors recommend patients take a daily stroll in the Sculpture Garden. The pleasure of enjoying the garden has become an inseparable everyday routine in the struggle for health.

01 | Ariel view of whole garden
02 | The crooked path creates a sense of concealment

03

04

05

03–05 | Sculptures in the garden encourage visitors to interact and connect with their surroundings, creating an uplifting, stimulating experience
06 | Ipe wooden seats provide additional rest stops

# Norma's Garden

LOCATION
Beechwood, USA

AREA
0.33 acre (0.13 hectare)

COMPLETION DATE
May 2005

LANDSCAPE DESIGN
Visionscapes/MKSK

BUDGET
US$725,000

PHOTOGRAPHY
MKSK

AWARDS
2006 Ohio Chapter American Society of Landscape Architects Merit Award

The Gathering Place is a caring community that supports, educates, and empowers individuals and families touched by cancer, through free programs and services. When the organization outgrew its existing space, the idea was born of establishing a healing garden to enable visitors to connect with nature. To initiate the process, Visionscapes worked with a facilitator to collect feedback from volunteers, cancer survivors, family members, and staff for creating the vision and program for the garden. MKSK, consulting landscape architects, were engaged to collaborate in the refinement of the master plan, to produce schematic, design development, and construction documents, as well as documents for securing municipal planning and zoning approvals. During construction, Visionscapes performed construction administration and on-site review for the client.

The Gathering Place offers programs of emotional support, gentle exercise, and a hands-on healing touch through a series of rooms providing small and large social areas, and acknowledgement of the four cardinal directions. Located in a commercial park on one-third of an acre (1335 square meters), Norma's Garden is an oasis of more than 123 species of trees, shrubs, perennials, grasses, and bulbs. Specifically designed to stimulate the senses, the garden features running water, rare textured plants, vibrant colorful flowers, scented blooming bulbs, edible flowers, herbs, and vegetables.

There are 10 distinct areas and garden rooms within the park, including the Entry and Walk of Friends, the Gathering Terrace and Portico, the Pool of Grass, the Pavilion, the Edible Garden, the Storybook Maze and the Sacred Mount, the Secret Mystery Garden, and the Green Rooms, offering intimate spaces for contemplation and reflection, raised beds for horticulture therapy programming, open play areas, and spaces for imaginative play. Challenges of the project included 13 feet (4 meters) of topographical change over one-third of the site, existing utilities, the commercial office warehouse site context and limited construction access. The garden was constructed with monetary and in-kind donations raised by the Gathering Place.

BLUEPRINT

Master plan

01

02

01 | The Secret Mystery Garden is a quiet place of respite and provides well-integrated ramps necessary to accommodate ADA access to the Sacred Mount

02 | The Walk of Friends entry to the garden with custom arbor and donor recognition art fence

03 | View from the Gathering Terrace to the Storybook Maze, pavilion and pool of grass
04 | The Children's Garden features sand play, the mole hill, a preserved and carved tree trunk log crawl, storytelling rock and splash pond
05 | Detail of the Water Leaves fountain, which enhances the Portico and entrance to the Green Rooms
06 | The Gathering Terrace, water element, and custom arbor

04

05

06

07 | The Storybook Maze, which tells a story of rebirth in the transformation of a caterpillar to a butterfly, traverses the hillside
08 | Water discovery within the Secret Mystery Garden
09 | The hillside stream springs from the Sacred Mount and terminates in a splash pool within the Children's Garden

08

09

Plan

03 | Aerial context view showing the Old City
04 | Pink axis

04

05 | Central area
06 | Pink axis
07 | Sensory planting

07

ⓐ Sensory planting
ⓑ Checkboard tress
ⓒ Fruit trees
ⓓ–ⓕ Pedrali outdoor furniture
ⓖ Artist planters

08 | Play area
09 | Children having fun with the furniture
10 | Visitors relax
11 | Central area

11

# Chang Gung Rehabilitation Hospital

LOCATION
Taoyuan, Taiwan, China

AREA
42 acres (17.5 hectares)

CLIENT
Ricky Liu & Associates

COMPLETION DATE
2008

LANDSCAPE DESIGN
McGregor Coxall Pty Ltd.

BUDGET
AU$7.5 million

PHOTOGRAPHY
Cheng Chin-Ming Photography

At the time of completion, the Taoyuan branch of Chang Gung Hospital was the single largest medical facility in the world, developed on a 43-acre (17.5-hectare) site by Formosa Plastics, owners of a number of private hospitals in Taiwan.

McGregor Coxall (then mcgregor+partners) was commissioned for site planning, design, construction documentation, and site review of the entire external works including green roofs. The facility has 3000 beds servicing both day surgery and a large percentage of patients who generally stay for periods longer than three months. The building is designed with flexible facilities and is expected to accommodate social and medical advancements well into the future.

The site program was conceived from the notion that landscape is important to the psychological and physical healing process of the patients. Design components included extensive roof gardens, a sunken courtyard café, interactive water features, walking trails, a sundial plaza, tea gardens, and outdoor art/craft workshop plazas.

The idea of using external space for recreation and relaxation in hospitals was not well accepted in Taiwan when the design was conceived in 1997. Credit is due to the local architects who realized that the facility needed international landscape expertise, and convinced the client to hire McGregor Coxall and set aside an appropriate budget. The client had not installed rooftop gardens in their previous hospitals, so initially the designers had to convince them that these were desirable environmental and social assets for the hospital.

The project has extremely advanced water-recycling capabilities. Maximum efficiency is achieved through water recycling and purification from the on-site sewage plant. The project is 100 percent water self-sufficient, and all non-potable water for the project is supplied through an on-site black-water treatment plant. McGregor Coxall also worked with engineers to change a traditional piped stormwater outlet from the building into a 98-foot-long (30-metre-long) cascading viaduct that empties into an elliptical wetland detention pond. Clean water leaving the pond enters a downstream creek.

BLUEPRINT

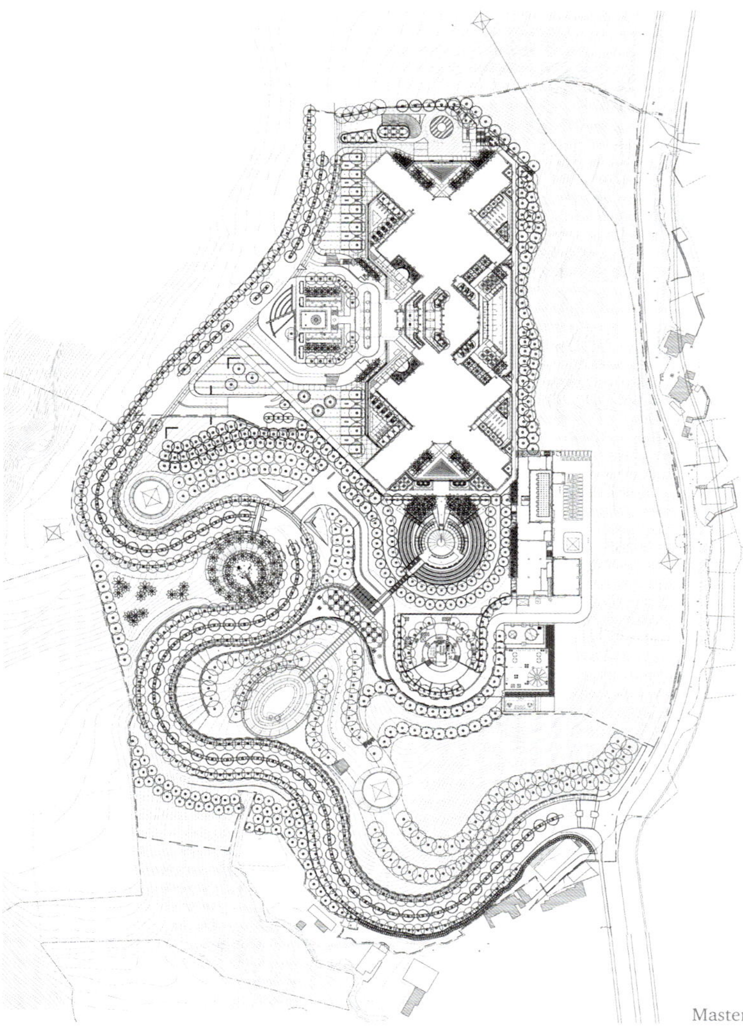

Master plan

Elevation

01 Building courtyards viewed from above show the variety of garden spaces available for both visitors and patients

02 | Entry courtyard details
03 | Entry plaza and courtyards viewed from above

04 | Entry plaza and courtyards viewed from above

05 | Entry plaza with sunken gardens
06 | Garden-viewing terraces adjoining wards overlooking the surrounding hillsides

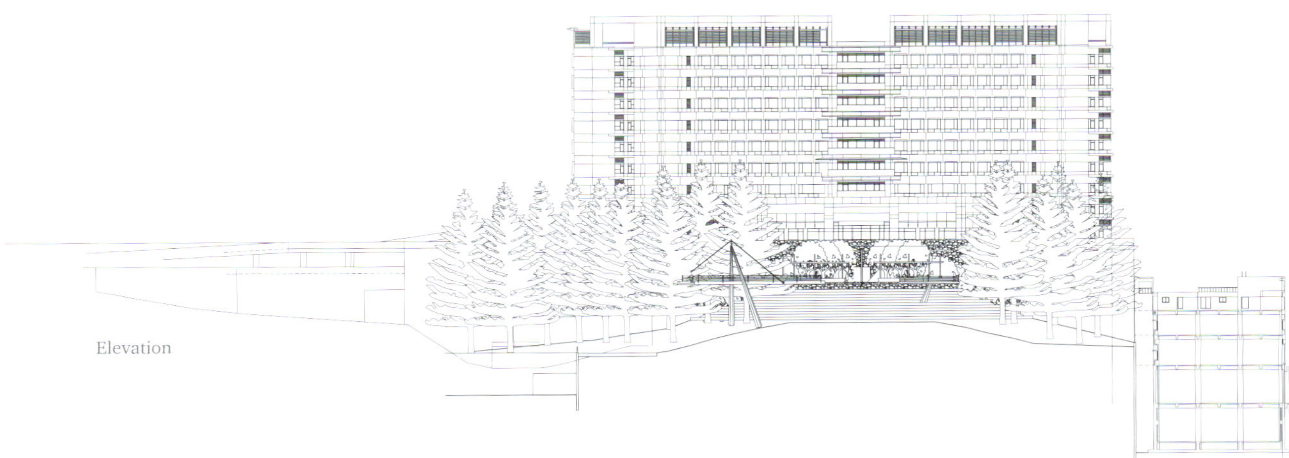

Elevation

07 | Entry plaza looking into the sunken garden

08 | Sundial plaza with arbor seating
09 | Entry road and pedestrian pathway
10 | One of the many planted courtyards
11 | Terraced garden and water collection weir and pond

# Toronto East General Hospital Garden

LOCATION
Toronto, Canada

AREA
2669 square feet (248 square meters)

CLIENT
Toronto East General Hospital Complex Continuing Care Unit

COMPLETION DATE
2003

LANDSCAPE DESIGN
Tales of the Earth

BUDGET
CA$600,000

PHOTOGRAPHY
Dennis Alan Winters

BLUEPRINT

The garden is an integral expression of the unit's vision statement, providing home in a safe, caring environment. Respecting and valuing residents and their support network, the Complex Continuing Care garden helps restore confidence through positive aging, offering both privacy and interaction with others.

Within a challenging space of 140 feet (42.7 meters) long and 9 to 23 feet (2.5 to 7 meters) wide, the garden was designed as a sculpture, stimulating all senses. The design vocabulary speaks to the richness and depth of historical and cultural traditions brought to the unit by residents from their varied birthplaces and homelands—Britain, Ireland, Greece, Italy, Sri Lanka, India, Vietnam, the Philippines, and China. The richness of spaces and details gives unique depth of character and meaning to the spirit of the garden that is like a little United Nations. Stimulating all senses, two richly colored steel pavilions fabricated by Magus Corporation of Lindsay, Ontario, frame the garden. The richness and depth of historically layered details, recalling structures of the residents' homelands, inspired the steel structure details without being historically redundant.

The dome of the light-blue temple at the south reflects similar spiritual sanctuaries where residents likely once sought refuge. The temple is for private, sheltered family visits. Underneath the garden's elegant dome, its oculus opens to the sky, allowing people to feel nestled and secure. The warmly colored dry-laid sandstone walls of the planting beds enclose the path. Weaving from one pavilion to the other, the path is wide enough for two wheelchairs to easily pass. It gently changes orientation like the seen and hidden technique of Japanese stroll gardens, so that it's experienced as something larger than it truly is, yet clearly defined so residents always know just where they are.

Next to the temple is the piazza, its shape inspired by the plan of Piazza Navonna in Rome. Within a pair of Tuscan-red semi-circular trellises in the middle of the piazza sits a shallow teal-blue tiled table pond. The pond is high enough for residents, sitting in their wheelchairs, to splash their fingers through the water.

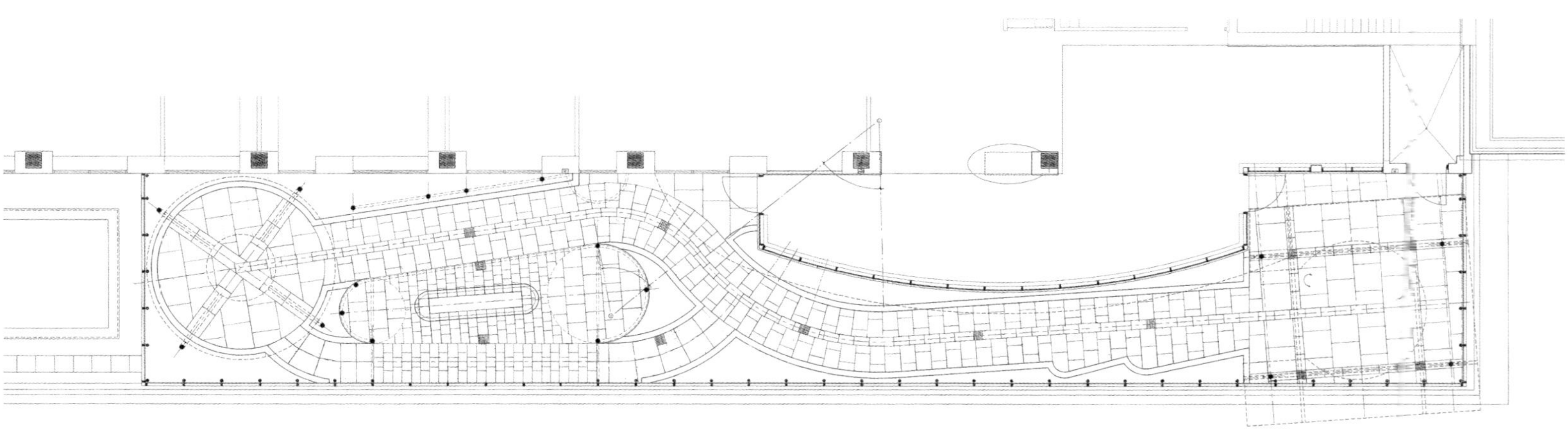

Site plan

01–02 | The road between stone planters is wide enough for two wheelchairs

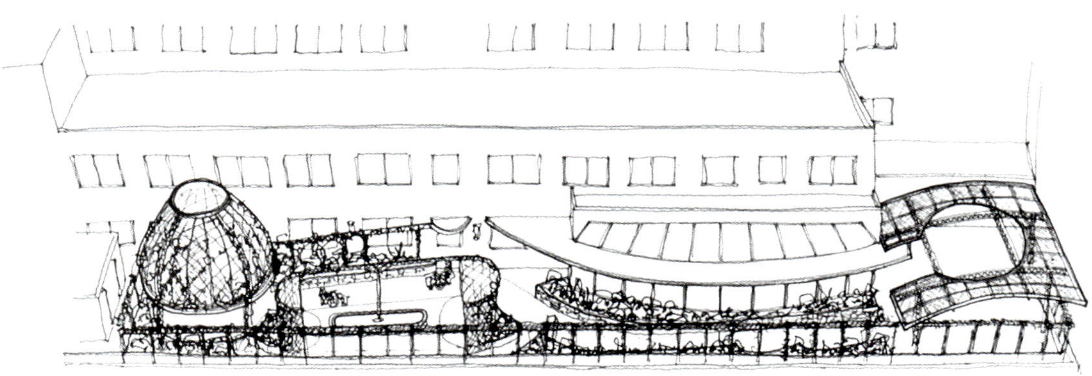

Bird's-eye sketch

03–04 | Mature native plants
05–07 | Local plants adapt well to the environment

06

# Los Angeles County + University of Southern California Medical Center

LOCATION
Los Angeles, USA

AREA
20 acres (8.09 hectares)

CLIENT
Los Angeles County + University of Southern California Medical Center

COMPLETION DATE
2008

LANDSCAPE DESIGN
Rios Clementi Hale Studios

PHOTOGRAPHY
Tom Bonner

In conceiving the landscape architecture for the new Los Angeles County + University of Southern California Medical Center (LAC + USC) site, Rios Clementi Hale Studios used large, bold, geometric patterns abstracted from regional history and geology. The design reinterprets and integrates elements and patterns from the new building and existing site throughout the campus. The result is a fluid and engaging conversation between structure, landscape, and community.

Rios Clementi Hale Studios' extensive site work encompasses automobile and pedestrian circulation systems, entry plazas, pedestrian thoroughfares and plazas, gardens, and the overall development and patterning of hardscape and planting. The design delineates a distinct identity for each individual element and its functional needs, and unifies them with a master plan that organically fits the building to its site.

An animated juxtaposition of circular and rectilinear shapes blankets the tiered ground plane like a Mexican tapestry, giving way to a mosaic of paving patterns and site features. Elements include a long grove of oak trees set diagonally to a curved lawn amphitheater. A ribbon-like ramp leads to a pedestrian walkway above.

BLUEPRINT

1. Chicago Street
2. Marengo Street
3. State Street
4. Outpatient building
5. Diagnostic and treatment building
6. Inpatient building
7. Central plant

01

Master plan

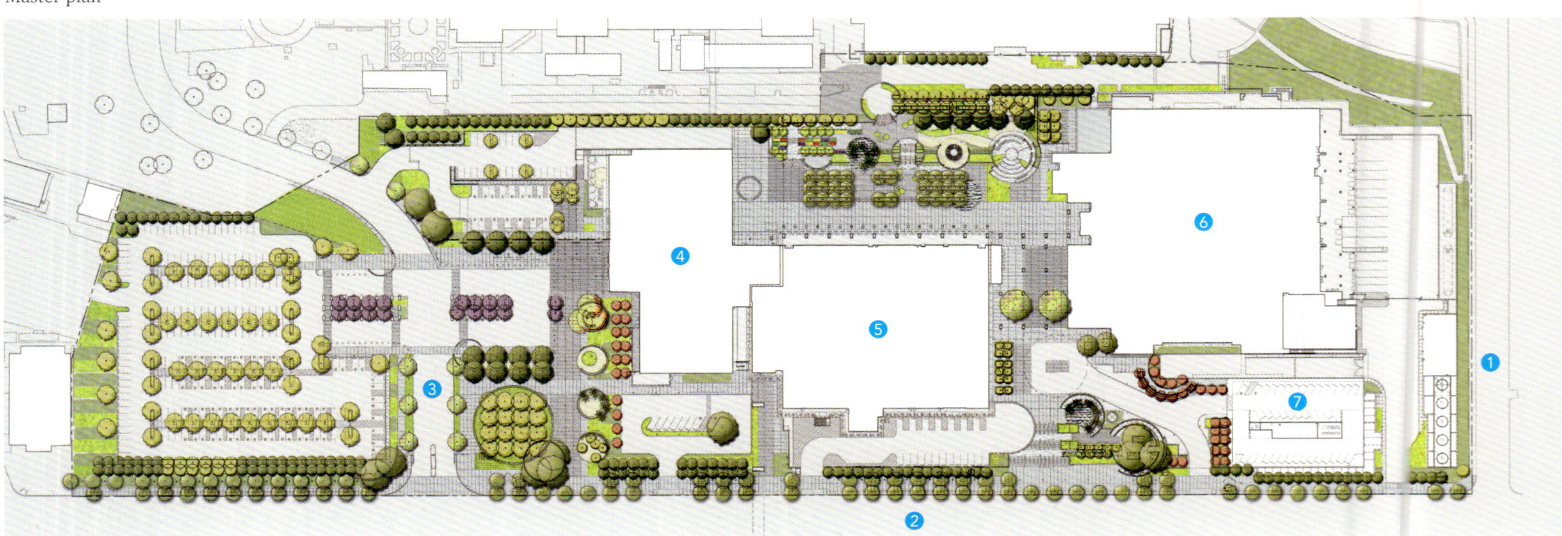

Refreshing bosques, colored concrete, sand-colored decomposed granite hardscape, drought-tolerant underplantings and shrubs, and seating areas and gardens of various sizes play into the overall pattern. The feeling is open and spacious, yet comfortably interconnected.

The landscape architecture further addresses 100 feet (30.5 meters) of elevation change across the 20 acres (81 hectares). At the site's lowest level, abstract wave-like patterns run through the concrete paving surface. At the high point, columnar Canary Island pine trees evoke the mountain peaks and vistas surrounding Los Angeles. Throughout, graceful lines, ramps, stairs, plazas, and walkways traverse the pedestrian-friendly topography.

Rios Clementi Hale Studios also designed a line of concrete and metal site furnishings expressly for LAC + USC's outdoor environs. The pieces are part of a system of repetitive forms and echo the overriding site design. Examples include the curved concrete benches that ring a series of circular meditation gardens, each planted in a distinct fashion. Nearby, a round, plant-free seating plaza is embedded with a ground design suggesting a meditative labyrinth. Other areas feature rows of rectangular concrete benches detailed with a slatted-wood treatment on the seating surfaces.

The narrative for the conceptual design of the project began with research into the existing L.A. County facility—where the Beaux Arts–style main building has long been an iconic fixture of the Los Angeles skyline—and the general history of the city and its inhabitants. Restored portions of the old hospital retained many of its original WPA terrazzo floors as well as tile murals depicting working-class families and agrarian life in early Los Angeles.

Further project research explored the varied geological formations native to the Los Angeles area, and Rios Clementi Hale Studios incorporated references from the mountains, the valley, and the coastline into the site design. Through this thematic work, the landscape architecture at the new LAC + USC site goes beyond anchoring the medical center to its immediate surroundings—it also connects the facility, and the people it serves, to Southern California's diverse natural environment.

01 | A grove of native oak trees provides sheltered seating on the main plaza
02 | Circular gardens of various sizes in the main plaza provide a range of outdoor experiences from meditation to children's play

03

04

03 | Gardens with custom benches line the entry drive below the historic main building
04 | Circular meditation garden with Chorisia speciosa
05 | Small circular planters showcase diverse flora along the courtyard walk
06 | Undulating seat wall forms edge to native garden

05

06

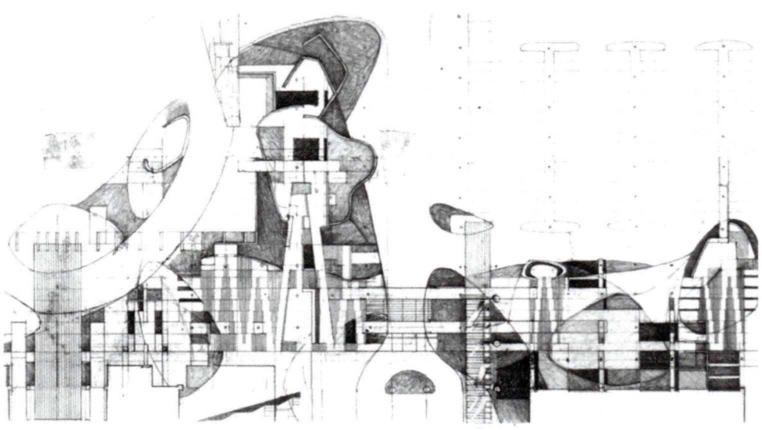

Section

07 | Circular garden with seating and meditative labyrinth

08 | The inner garden courtyard with circular gardens provides a quiet landscape setting for the busy hospital complex

09 | Circular gardens provide seating along the entry walk

10 | The Garden of the Senses incorporates tiered planters to allow for touching and smelling the plants

# Capital Health Medical Center

LOCATION
Hopewell Township, USA

AREA
166 acres (67.17 hectares)

CLIENT
Ocean Medical Center

COMPLETION DATE
2011

LANDSCAPE DESIGN
Sikora Wells Appel

BUDGET
US$15 million

PHOTOGRAPHY
Sikora Wells Appel

The 320-bed, LEED Gold Capital Health Medical Center is nestled in a 166-acre (67.2-hectare) site surrounded by woodlands, wetlands and drainage ways. Envisioned as a holistic healing environment, the grounds incorporate a number of outdoor spaces including three roof gardens: two extensive roofs for viewing, and a therapeutic roof garden that provides both viewing interest and allows patients, visitors, and staff to rejuvenate in a garden setting.

The overall site has been developed to promote good land stewardship through the use of state-of-the-art land and stormwater management practices. The site, with the exception of the more formally executed garden areas adjacent to the hospital, is designed to be seen as an extension of the existing natural landscape. Large expanses of open land are planted and maintained as native meadow. Stormwater will be channeled through artificial bioswales and wetlands, designed to simulate natural features and provide critical bio-habitat, and engineered to maximize percolation/management of on-site runoff. Rainwater collected from the roof is stored underground in four 10,000-gallon cisterns and reused for irrigation.

The site immediately surrounding the hospital is more 'gardenesque' in design and includes a series of garden rooms connected by a continuous pathway. These outdoor spaces provide not only the opportunity for rest, relaxation, and reflection but, depending on their location, function as play area, dining space, informal gathering/meeting room, waiting room and, inherent to all, gardens that promote and inspire healing.

The specific gardens include the following:

1. The Women's and Children's Garden: a fanciful walled garden with chalk wall, curvy pavement designs, and colorful evening lighting.
2. The Café Garden: an outdoor dining space with splashing fountain, bluestone paving, and fragrant rose hedge.

BLUEPRINT

① Entrace
② Proposed main drive
③ Van Pincis Road
④ Proposed loop road
⑤ Meadow planting
⑥ Constructed wetlands basin
⑦ Parking
⑧ Patient discharge
⑨ Proposed phase 2 bed tower
⑩ Main entrance
⑪ CHS hospital/medical office
⑫ Emergency entrance, ambulances only
⑬ Emergency entrance, walk-in
⑭ Proposed loading area
⑮ Central utility plant
⑯ Cancer treatment entrance
⑰ Proposed phase 2 parking
⑱ Existing wetlands
⑲ Sewage pump station

Master Plan

3. The Cancer Treatment Garden: a contemplation garden with arbor, water runnel, and colorful garden plantings.
4. The Board Room Gardens: outdoor rooms for informal meetings and socializing; amenities include lighted arbors, decorative bollard lighting, and fragrant rose hedging.
5. The Conference Courtyard: a semi-walled, shaded 'break-out' space paved in bluestone for socializing/relaxing and enjoying the sounds from the surrounding fountain wall.
6. The Emergency Walk-In Garden: a shaded outdoor waiting area adjacent to the emergency room.
7. The Patient Discharge Garden: an oval-shaped outdoor waiting room and contemplative garden set among shade-loving plants and flowering magnolia trees.
8. The Second-Story Roof Garden: a landscaped healing garden accessible from the cancer treatment rooms; amenities include shade arbor with seating, wood deck with seating, and ornamental plantings.

01 | Cancer Treatment Garden
02 | The healing garden provides a contemplative space for visitors and staff to enjoy the many seating options available

① Existing 'moraine' honey locust
② Mixed perennials
③ Existing 'Greenspire' linden
④ Evergreen groundcover
⑤ 'Big blue' liriope
⑥ Existing 'Big blue' liriope
⑦ Existing amelanchier 'cumulus'
⑧ Existing clethra 'hummingbird' and 'happy returns' daylily
⑨ Wet-tolerant perennials
⑩ Mixed perennials
⑪ Annual display
⑫ Base bid: mown lawn
Add alternate: exposed aggregate concrete
⑬ Flowering perennial
⑭ Ornamental grass
⑮ Evergreen groundcover
⑯ Mixed drought-tolerant perennials in stone bed

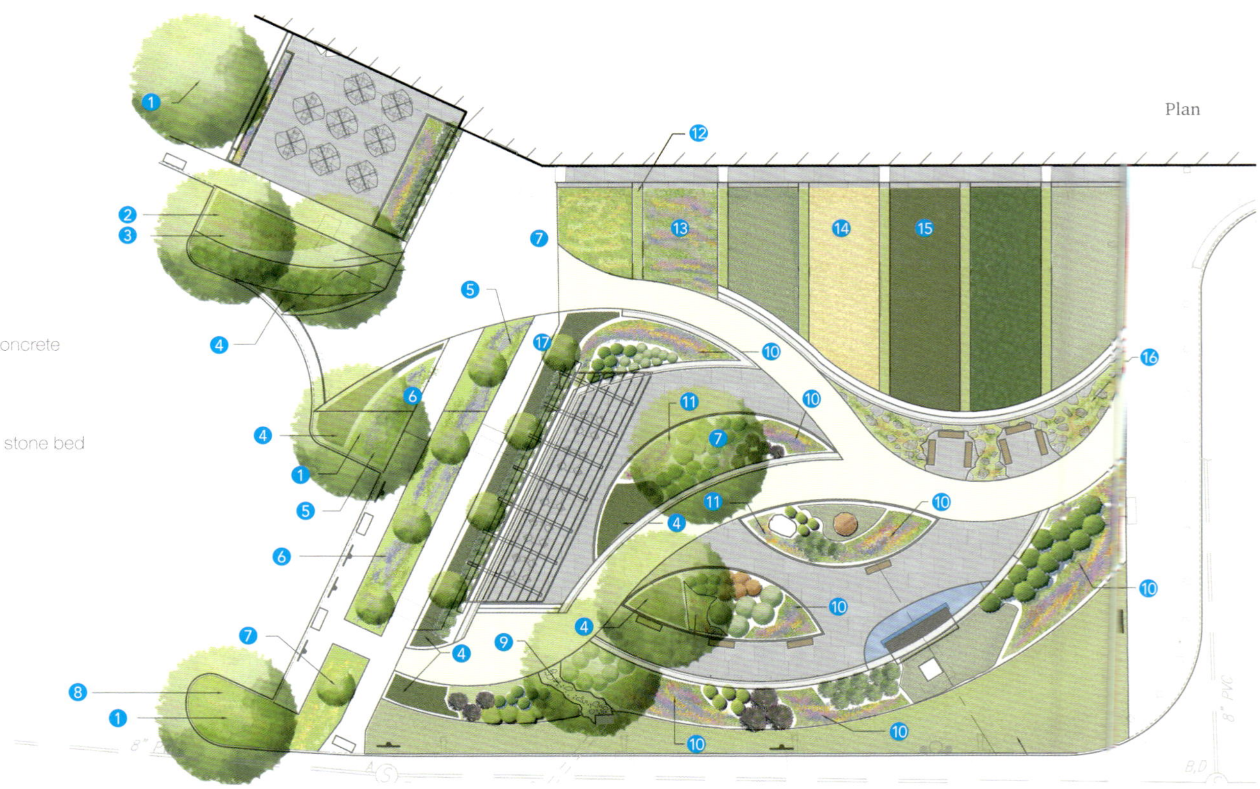


03 | Stone-lined runnel allows water to fall into a stainless-steel canister
04 | The second-floor roof garden is landscaped with sweeping pathways

05 | View of a roof garden illustrates the variety and beauty of the garden's planting and circular walkway
06 | In the café garden, users are surrounded by lush, colorful planting and a simple water feature

# Elizabeth & Nona Evans Restorative Garden

LOCATION
Cleveland, USA

AREA
8400 square feet (780.39 square metres)

CLIENT
Cleveland Botanical Garden

COMPLETION DATE
2004

LANDSCAPE DESIGN
Dirtworks Landscape Architecture, PC

PHOTOGRAPHY
Randall Schieber, Nick Fancher

AWARD
2014 International Awards for Universal Design Silver Award, Japan
2006 American Society of Landscape Architects (ASLA) Honor Award in General Design
2008 British Holistic Medical Association Design Commendation, United Kingdom
2006 American Society of Landscape Architects (ASLA) New York Chapter Honor Award in General Design
2006 American Society of Landscape Architects (ASLA) Ohio Chapter Merit Award in General Design
2006 American Horticultural Therapy Association (AHTA) Honor Award, Therapeutic Garden Design

The Elizabeth and Nona Evans Restorative Garden is an integral part of the Cleveland Botanical Garden's mission to 'blend education, social responsibility, cultural and environmental stewardship' to help people of all ages, backgrounds, and abilities appreciate and benefit from the positive role that plants play in their lives. The Restorative Garden offers a diverse plant collection in a series of three unique settings, each with a distinct character and level of activity: for quiet contemplation; for individual exploration and teaching groups; and for horticultural therapy. Most importantly, the garden does these things discreetly and comfortably, for people of all abilities.

The Contemplative Garden, a verdant elegant space adjacent to the garden's library, serves as the entry point for the entire Restorative Garden. A reflecting pool with a fountain muffles nearby noises. The space features a wheelchair-accessible lawn panel contained by a stone walk. The custom-designed handrail accommodates arthritic hands and also incorporates poems in Braille. Color in this calm setting is muted—primarily shades of green. Flowers and fragrances are also minimized. To accommodate the site's significant grade change, a stone retaining wall anchors one side of the garden.

The Demonstration/Exploration Garden is another space with an unusual sense of intimacy and privacy, accommodating both individual exploration and group activities. A low retaining wall is a participatory feature offering a variety of sensory opportunities for touching, smelling, and hearing. Carefully selected stones, interesting plants, and water features engage users, whether sitting or standing, and also mask nearby traffic noise. Plants cascade over the wall and grow in niches, encouraging visitors to stretch and explore, which helps develop motor skills. The canopy of a featured tree captures moisture from one of the water features, creating a cool, inviting microclimate.

The Horticultural Therapy Garden is sunny, dynamic, and overflowing with sensory interest. Visitors, some with severe disabilities, are offered a choice of planter widths and heights for ease of use and carefully selected plants for individual abilities. A dozen varieties of basil provide a long growing season, and plants are of various heights and blooms, so everyone is catered for—whether walking or sitting in wheelchairs. Paths, activity areas, and a welcome area are all spacious. Planter walls and a berm ensure privacy between adjacent spaces, so the public can enjoy this garden without intruding or distracting group activities.

BLUEPRINT

A series of distinct 'garden rooms', are planned within the context of the existing botanical garden

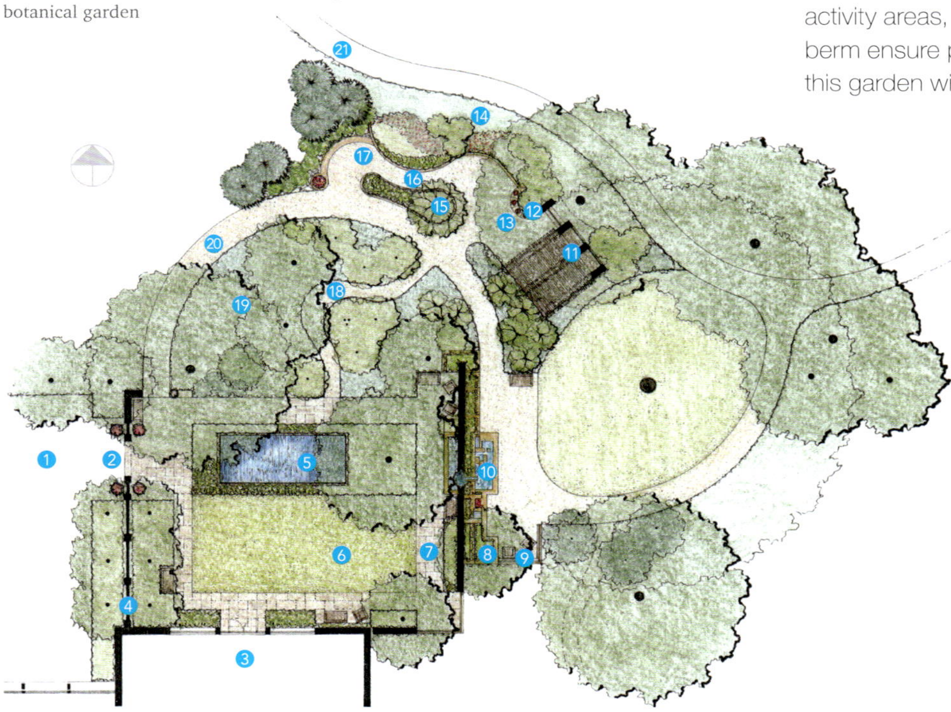

1. Terrace
2. Entry
3. Stone wall
4. Reflecting pool
5. Lawn panel
6. Lookout with Braille rail
7. A garden for contemplation
8. Shade garden
9. Lookout with Braille rail
10. Demonstration wall with featured plantings, water elements, and stone
11. Trellis and storage
12. Stepped planters
13. Group activities
14. Perennial embankment
15. Raised planters for therapy and display
16. Sensory walk
17. Welcome area
18. 'Secret' path
19. 'Hidden' garden
20. Main path
21. Public walk

01

02

01 | Horticultural therapy programs are integrated with plants and landform so privacy is achieved without being isolated from the surrounding garden

02 | A stone retaining wall, featuring cascading plants and water features, defines separate areas of the garden

03 | Compositions of water, plants, and walls create distinct garden experiences
04 | The contemplative garden features a lawn panel that supports wheelchairs without the need for in-ground structural reinforcement
05 | Paths take visitors by features that are interesting to hear and touch
06 | Lookouts, providing views and a place to pause, have custom-designed railings to accommodate arthritic hands

07 | The Horticultural Therapy Garden is entered through a large welcome area, placed out of the main circulation
08 | The wall is laid with interesting local stone interspersed with fragrant, richly textured plants that invite touching and smelling
09 | The rails are designed with Braille inserts that incorporate a changing collection of poems
10 | Framed by soft textured plants, water trickles over a moss-covered stone niche in the wall
11 | Path gradients are calculated to minimize fatigue and to provide subtle places to pause, rest, and enjoy a focal point

12 | Movable benches and chairs promote comfortable, flexible seating areas with varying degrees of privacy for individuals and groups

# Healing Garden at the Life Enrichment Center

LOCATION
Kings Mountain, USA

AREA
1.15 acres (0.4 hectares)

CLIENT
Life Enrichment Center

COMPLETION DATE
2004

LANDSCAPE DESIGN
Dirtworks Landscape Architecture, PC

PHOTOGRAPHY
Bruce Buck

BLUEPRINT

Site plan. The garden comprises three distinct spaces that vary in size, complexity, physical demand, and degree of sensory engagement

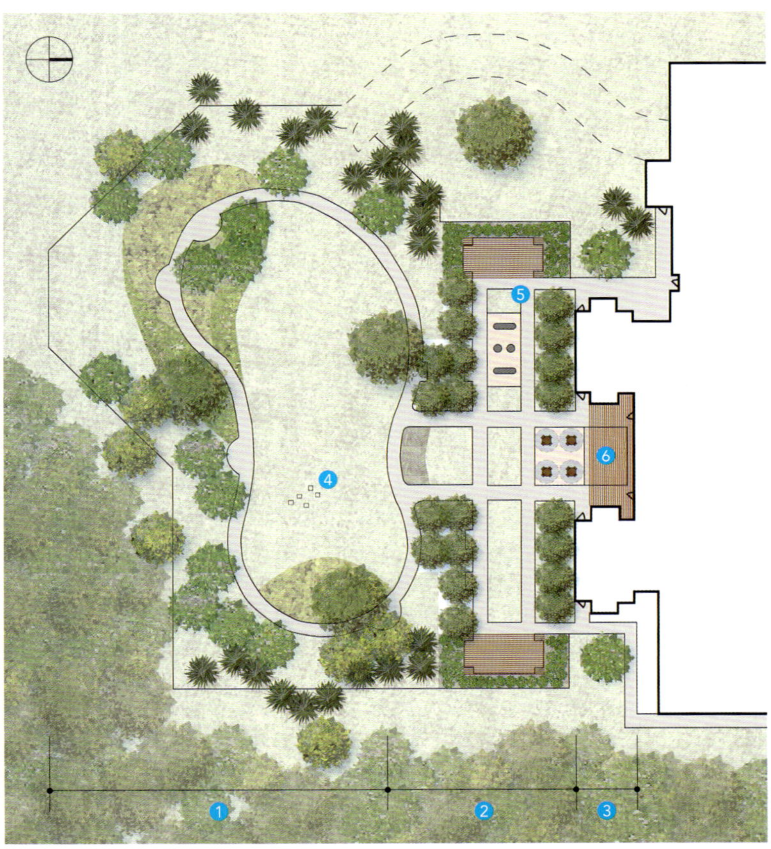


The Life Enrichment Center is located in the foothills of the North Carolina Mountains. It is a sustainable community-based Adult Day Care facility, serving adults of all ages with a range of physical and mental disabilities and neurological conditions. The center's philosophy is to do whatever it takes to help families keep adult loved ones at home and engaged in their community.

Enriching and supporting a dignified quality of life is never more poignant than when that life involves degenerative disease. Complex neurological conditions, including Alzheimer's disease, require concepts of treatment that incorporate both pharmacological as well as non-pharmacological approaches. Medications, the first and often last step in treatment, offer meager solace for people who live daily with these conditions. Like other chronic illnesses that require lifestyle changes, such as diabetes, manic depression and AIDS, Alzheimer's requires a model of care beyond medication that emphasizes living with existing abilities.

One such care modality can be a physical environment that promotes safety and reduces fear by directing cognition even without the person's awareness. It involves a designed environment that helps people find their way, engages them, and jogs their memory. The therapeutic settings provided within this supportive environmental design facilitate activities that compensate for cognitive defects.

Dirtworks Landscape Architecture, PC was tasked with developing an outdoor setting that would complement the center's varied programs of care. Emphasizing both individual and environmental health, the 1.15-acre (0.4-hectare) garden implements a number of sustainable components including an integrated pest-management system and organic garden. Accommodating the range of cognitive abilities and complex medical conditions required close collaboration with the managers and staff in programming, design, and construction. The staff and Dirtworks Landscape Architecture, PC's interest in emerging investigations within cognitive science informed the specifics of the design.

The resulting garden is comprised of three distinct spaces that vary in size, complexity, physical demand, and degree of sensory engagement. Its deceptively simple overall aesthetic belies complex considerations. The garden's basic elements, including domestic-scaled structures and spaces, native plants, and local fruits, vegetables and herbs, are familiar to residents who have lived their entire lives in this agricultural region. The experience is therefore understandable and manageable. Seen cohesively, the garden offers opportunities and choices for everyone, regardless of ability, to engage with nature on their own terms, in their own way and at their own pace.

① Park
② Promenade
③ Porch
④ Expansive lawn, sweeps of native plants, bird feeders, and views of the surrounding woodlands
⑤ Framed by flowering trees, the promenade is highlighted by trellises and planters
⑥ The climate-controlled porch modulates sunlight and features a raised fireplace

01 | Framed by native trees and grasses, a path-surrounded lawn area provides a familiar and safe venue for those with dementia
02 | Spacious seating areas along a meandering path offer privacy and views of the surrounding woodlands

Garden design section showing the park, promenade and porch

03 | The garden trellises provide shade for activities and casual socializing. Beyond the garden trellises, patients can participate in more physically interactive and challenging activities on the lawn
04 | Spacious seating areas along a meandering path offer privacy and views of the surrounding woodlands
05 | A looped pathway with familiar landmarks, sounds and smells help residents with Alzheimer's avoid confusion and enjoy the different garden spaces while keeping clear sight lines to the Life Enrichment Center
06 | Morning routines, such as checking bird feeders for adequate seed supply, provide pleasant and useful opportunities for exercise and strengthening motor-coordination skills

04

05

06

07

08

09

10

11

Garden design section showing
the promenade and porch

① Porch
② Promenade

07 | The promenade is anchored by two vine-covered trellises that serve as orientation landmarks. Flowers, herbs and fruit, grown in planters, accommodate varying levels of interest and ability

08 | A vine-covered trellis, providing dappled shade, helps create a comfortable transition between indoor and outdoor spaces

09 | A raised planter, accessible from both sides, allows individuals with physical limitations to participate in tending the garden and the opportunity to socialize

10 | A favorite spot for casual gatherings and programmed activities, the porch has ceiling fans and a raised fireplace to provide a comfortable, climate-controlled space year-round

11 | Clear sight lines from the living room to the porch to the garden create a sense of welcome and help to invite residents to enjoy the garden

# Miami Valley Hospital Respite Gardens

LOCATION
Dayton, USA

AREA
109 acres (44.11 hectares)

CLIENT
Premier Health Partners

COMPLETION DATE
2010

LANDSCAPE DESIGN
NBBJ

PHOTOGRAPHY
Sean Airhart

BLUEPRINT

Miami Valley Hospital Respite Gardens acts as an oasis for patients and tired staff. Patients, in particular, reap the benefits of this peaceful garden environment, which offers both physical and psychological recuperative effects.

As part of the transformation of the Miami Valley Hospital's downtown facility, which included the construction of the handsome new 12-story Heart Center, the existing main entrance and associated open space were demolished to make way for a new vehicular arrival court and a new arrival garden, a striking addition to this well-established facility.

For the hundreds of daily visitors, the arrival court provides a comfortable space, adjacent to the hospital lobby, to drop off and pick up throughout the day. Once in the parking structure, visitors have the option of taking a direct path to the hospital under a covered pergola, or strolling through the arrival garden to reach the front door. The garden features a graceful meandering path with a bridge over the garden stream. Shade and ornamental trees define smaller spaces within the garden, while groundcovers and flower beds provide texture and color to the landscape. A patio space at the northern edge of the garden provides benches as well as tables and chairs, inviting family, friends, and co-workers to enjoy the relaxing environment.

In addition to the gardens at ground level, there's a green-roof garden on the third level of the hospital, designed for viewing from the upper-level patient rooms, with a pattern of colorful plantings and paver pathways. The roof garden serves as both a visual feature and a sustainable solution, as the insulation provided by the roof plantings reduces glare and energy costs, and improves stormwater runoff.

1. New central courtyard with staff patio, water feature, walks, and bridge
2. New main entry with drop-off, canopy, and landscape island
3. Stone retaining walls with integral water feature
4. Green-roof system

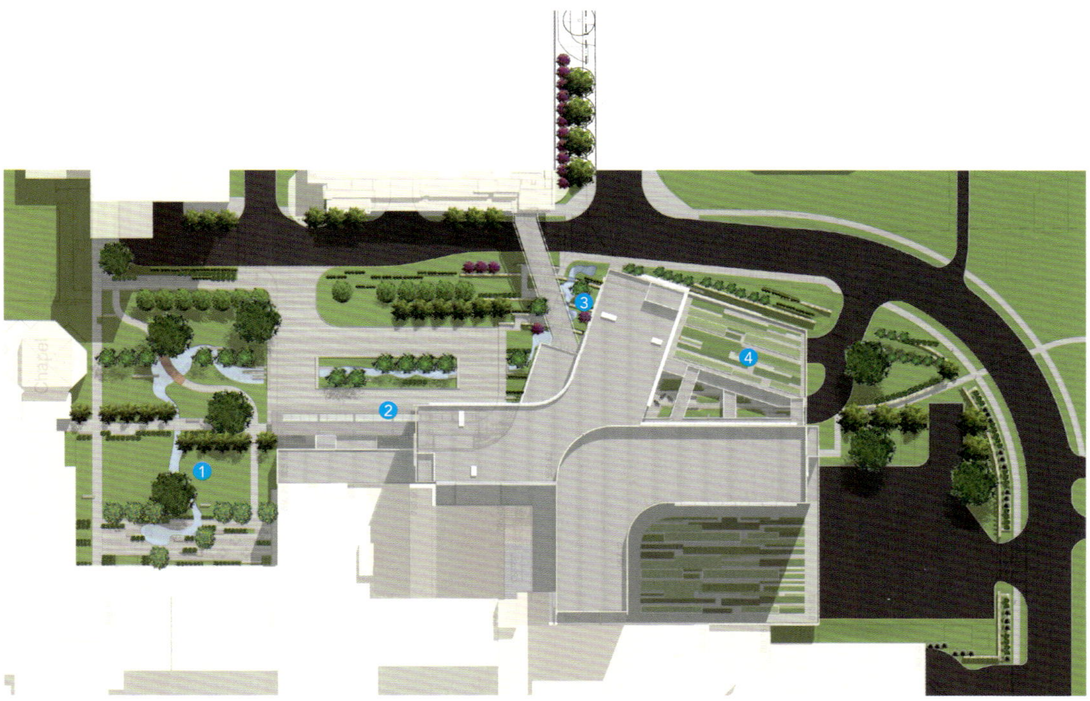


Master plan

01 | The respite garden becomes the foreground for the new Heart Center tower
02 | New pathways passing through the gardens connect parking areas to the new Heart Center front door

03 | The new Heart Center tower, arrival court, and respite garden reimagine the medical center
04 | Waterfalls penetrate limestone retaining walls located at the main medical center drive and the new arrival plaza
05 | The new green roof consists of a variety of sedum varieties, with paths for access and a patterned composition

06 | View from the upper levels of the Heart Center tower look down on intimate outdoor courtyards as well as a 10,764-square-foot (1000-square-meter) green roof

10

11

07 | Courtyards on upper floors encourage staff and visitors to enjoy the outdoors; trees and plants with texture and color accent the spaces
08 | Finely crafted limestone walls allow access from the new arrival plaza to walkways below, and offer places of relaxation
09 | Waterfalls penetrate limestone retaining walls located the main medical center drive and the new arrival plaza
10 | The respite garden is a series of spaces that make up the larger space and provide places for patients, staff, and visitors to retreat and relax
11 | Staff enjoy a break in one of the upper-level courtyards

# Horatio's Garden

LOCATION
Salisbury, UK

AREA
0.27 acres (1100 square metres)

CLIENT
Horatio's Garden registered charity

COMPLETION DATE
2012

LANDSCAPE DESIGN
Cleve West

BUDGET
£300,000

PHOTOGRAPHY
Cleve West, Olivia Chapple

AWARDS
2014 Commercial or Public Space Award, People's Choice Award and Judges' Award, Society of Garden Designer Awards

Horatio's Garden was designed for the Duke of Cornwall Spinal Treatment Center as a peaceful, recuperative environment for the patients who had experienced spinal cord injury. Landscape designer Cleve West was asked to create a beautiful sanctuary as a patients' retreat from an austere clinical environment. But there were a lot of practical considerations as well. The garden needed to be accessible by hospital beds and wheelchairs. There needed to be private areas and communal areas, somewhere for garden therapy, and for wildlife.

The project was started by Horatio Chapple, an aspiring doctor and a volunteer on the spinal unit. He was surprised that there was nowhere for the patients to get outside during their long stays in hospital, so he used a simple questionnaire to find out what sort of garden patients would enjoy. Tragically, Horatio was killed by a polar bear on an Arctic expedition in August 2011. A fund was set up to create the garden, and trustees proposed that it should be called Horatio's Garden.

The garden is a symbol of the love and hope that can come out of tragedy. Cleve West built on Horatio's research by consulting with patients, staff, hospital managers, and therapists before coming up with his design. He had an understanding of the needs of the project, because his best friend had suffered a spinal cord injury 12 years before and had been a patient in the spinal center.

Low-lying limestone walls are the main feature of the garden. They course their way through the planting, creating a gentle structure that echoes the distant views of hills. These symbolise the journey that patients make while learning to live with paralysis, and represent hope for the future. Resin-bonded aggregate was used to form the paths and communal areas. This surface is totally smooth so that patients in beds can easily be wheeled into the garden, and patients using wheelchairs can access the space unaided.

BLUEPRINT

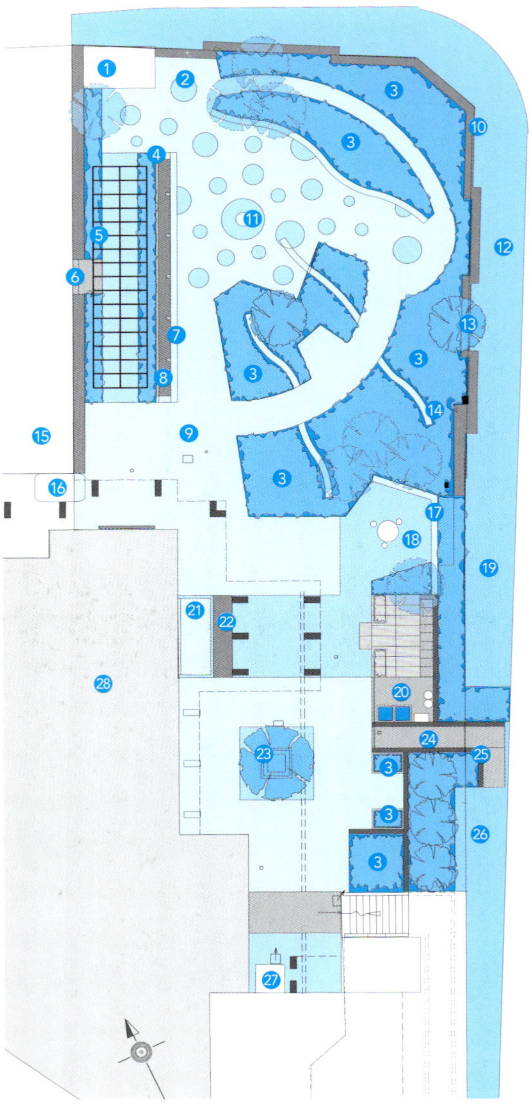

Master plan

1. Summer house
2. Circles of resin-bonded aggregate
3. Mixed planting with loose Buxus sempirvirens balls
4. Rill with flowing water
5. Steel archway
6. Oak gates with 'Horatio's Garden' carved in them
7. Walls with coping stones
8. Apple trees
9. Resin-bonded aggregate
10. Mixed native hedge
11. Memorial Stone to Horatio Chapple
12. Wildflower bank
13. Betula nigra–multistem (River birch) trees
14. Low limestone walls
15. Tennis court
16. Entrance gate
17. Limestone retaining wall
18. Gaze Burvill seating area carved with 'Horatio's Garden'
19. Hartley Botanic greenhouse
20. Composting area
21. Kitchen area
22. Garden room
23. Koelreuteria paniculata–Golden rain tree
24. Access path
25. Grass bank
26. Sesleria autumnalis and digitalis ferrugunea
27. Raised beds for therapeutic gardening
28. Spinal unit gym

The walls were created from reclaimed Cotswold stone by stone artist David Wilson. He created an unusual drystone pattern, finishing some of the walls with coping stones to act as seating for relatives and friends. Plants were carefully chosen to ensure the garden is beautiful throughout the year, with perennials combined with box balls, amelanchier and river birch trees. Masses of bulbs herald spring, and dahlias keep color in the garden until the frosts of autumn. A rill brings the calming sound of water and a large metal archway creates a tunnel of white wisteria for patients to lie underneath. Different varieties of trees of eating apples are planted in cordons over the arch.

Hartley Botanic supplied a beautiful greenhouse, with staging at the correct height for wheelchairs, and automated doors for easy access for patients with limited mobility. Gaze Burvill created an oak table and benches for patients and their relatives to use. Bespoke raised oak planters were designed to be moveable, enabling patients to work on them easily. A cutting area serves to supply flowers, which are cut for the patients' dining room. Salads, herbs and soft fruit are grown in raised beds, so they are easy to harvest for patients.

The garden is fitted with a watering system, and lighting creates a stunning nighttime spectacle for patients to enjoy from their wards. Bird boxes are fitted in the hedges with wireless webcams to screen in the ward. Butterflies and bees feast on the flowers' nectar, and birds sing from the trees. Horatio's Garden is a place of sanctuary, tears and laughter—but, above all, it's a place of hope.

01 | View of the spinal unit with the garden in summer
02 | The archway with wisteria floribunda 'alba' and espaliers of eating apples, underplanted with Libertia grandiflora

03 | Verbena bonariensis floats in the summer breeze
04 | Dawn on a June morning with Aruncus dioicus 'Horatio' in the foreground

05 | Bench designed by Cleve West
06 | Bird bath by sculptor Will Spankie
07 | The view to the Clarendon Way

08 | 'Erythrocyte' by sculptor David Worthington
09 | Gaze Burvill bench and table with sculpture by Rebecca Newnham
10 | Grasses Stipa gigantea

11 | Low limestone walls by stone artist David Wilson

12 | Gernaium Bill Wallace
13 | Stachys byzantina
14 | Centranthus ruber
15 | Allium christophii
16 | Tulipa Angelique and Recreado
17 | Sculpture 'Rose Deer' by Mark Coreth
18 | Echinachea purpurea 'White Swan'

19 | Erigeron karvinskianus tumbles from the walls
20 | View from the cutting garden towards the Hartley Botanic greenhouse
21 | Malus 'Laxton's Superb' ripening

22 | Aerial view when the garden first opened
23 | A patient working on wheelchair skills with a therapist

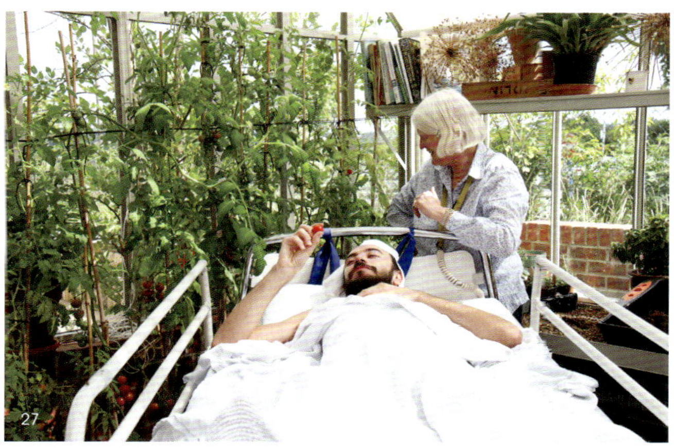

24 | Artist-in-residence Miranda Creswell works with a patient
25 | Patients in beds can enjoy the garden
26 | Artists-in-residence work regularly in the garden
27 | Volunteer helps a patient to pick tomatoes in the greenhouse

# Max Tanenbaum Healing Garden

LOCATION
Toronto, Canada

AREA
2442 square feet (227 square meters)

CLIENT
Princess Margaret Cancer Centre at University Health Network, Toronto

COMPLETION DATE
2014

LANDSCAPE DESIGN
Janet Rosenberg & Studio Inc.

BUDGET
CA$700,000

PHOTOGRAPHY
Debbie Gordon
Janet Rosenberg & Studio Inc.
Princess Margaret Hospital News
Overstreet Photography
Princess Margaret Cancer Foundation
System 4 Productions Inc.

BLUEPRINT

Perspective rendering

The Max Tanenbaum Healing Garden in Toronto's Princess Margaret Cancer Centre occupies a courtyard on the 14th floor and is directly visible off the elevator lobby on its northern end. The courtyard area is approximately 2442 square feet (227 square meters), and is centrally located with views available from patient rooms on three sides. The space is open above to the 16th floor as well as below through a centrally located skylight, and the garden surrounds the perimeter of the skylight.

Natural forms inspire a design consisting entirely of artificial materials, creating a colorful yet no-maintenance space. Delicate hand-blown glass flowers in bountiful colors and shapes create a beautiful textured canvas, set within a frame of boxwood parterres that surround the central skylight. The reference to cultivated 17th-century French parterres evokes an ornate, formal garden. Laser-cut screen panels on the walls, modeled on trimmed hedges, reinforce the courtyard as a room in the sky offering garden views and suspended disbelief. As the project evolved, an adjoining lobby was added to the scope, with floor-to-ceiling glass windows, allowing patients, family members, and staff to relax on comfortable furniture while enjoying views of the courtyard. Most importantly, the rich colors and natural forms have created a symbol of the perpetual blooming of hope and renewal.

Stringent weight restrictions exist in the courtyard, there is no access to water, and minimal access is provided for maintenance only. The parterres are therefore created with 2-foot-high (60-centimeter-high) artificial boxwoods, set within metal frames. These components are increasingly popular in gardens as a simple-to-install lightweight kit of parts. The boxwood is fireproof and stable to ultraviolet light. As the project evolved, the plan of the parterres was carried to the adjoining lobby by inserting the pattern in the wood floor.

The uplifting painterly design highlights flowers as symbols of the rhythms of nature as well as the predicament of winter in our own daily lives. For the Princess Margaret Cancer Centre, the glass artist Jenn Wanless-Craig (of Fuel Glassworks) assigned a name and a 'type' (two bulbs, two bowls, three petals, three panicles, and a single leaf) for each flower, conveying perpetual bounty, vigor, and hope as the inspirational pulse. Traditional western associations were referenced, such as the rose for love, lily for purity, and the sunflower for devotion. Each type requires a specific process to make, yet all flowers are attached to a long stainless-steel stem. The key, however, is color inspired by flower symbolism common in the Victorian era. The flowers are grouped by color within the compartments for greater effect, and hover about 2 feet (60 centimeters) above the French parterres. A poem in colors has been created, with areas of pink for compassion, purple for strength, red for courage, orange for dignity, yellow for perseverance, green for good fortune, and blue for gratitude. At night, point lights create a comforting, subtle, star-like effect.

The courtyard is a space designed for patients, as well as families and staff, to enjoy year-round, with measurable benefits to patient outcomes and staff satisfaction. The healing garden not only provides colorful, restful views for patients and staff, but doubles as a tribute to the many patients who have been affected by cancer. Families and friends can purchase one of the colorful glass flowers to dedicate to a loved one. By involving the community, the garden will grow over time with future donations.

01 | Purple glassy flowers
02 | Panorama view of the whole healing courtyard garden

Glass-flowers concept drawings

- ⓐ Green symbolizes good fortune
- ⓑ Purple and blue asters represent strength and health
- ⓒ Red protea represents courage
- ⓓ Yellow Euphorbia represents persistence
- ⓔ Pink heath represents solitude
- ⓕ Orange dahlia represents dignity
- ⓖ White dogwood represents hope

03–07 | All the glass flowers symbolize 'hope'

08 | Patients can enjoy the sight of the garden from indoors
09 | View from upstairs

10

11

12

13

14

10 | The rich colors of all the glass flowers create a symbol of the perpetual blooming of hope and renewal

11–13 | Warm-toned glass flowers

14 | Cool-toned glass flowers

# Chlois G. Ingram Spirit of Women Park

LOCATION
Columbus, USA

AREA
6 acres (2.43 hectares)

CLIENT
The Wexner Medical Center at The Ohio State University

COMPLETION DATE
2012

LANDSCAPE DESIGN
MKSK/OLIN

BUDGET
US$4.13 million

PHOTOGRAPHY
Randall Schieber, Nick Fancher

AWARDS
2013 American Society of Landscape Architects (ASLA) Ohio Chapter Merit Award

BLUEPRINT

As part of the first phase of implementation for the Wexner Medical Center expansion project at the Ohio State University (OSU), an existing park space has been relocated and reinvented with the goal of honoring the lives of women. Named for Chlois G. Ingram, a dedicated American Red Cross volunteer at OSU's Medical Center, the original Spirit of Women Park told personal stories and honored extraordinary women in their roles as mothers, grandmothers, sisters, nieces, friends, teachers, healers, and mentors through colorful, hand-painted tiles mounted on concrete walls between cascades of water.

The original concept to reuse the artwork from the former park proved difficult due to weathering and the fragility of the original ceramic tiles. Therefore, each tile was individually photographed and digitally traced to maintain the handmade quality of the original art. The donor tiles have now been given new life, with 1515 etched glass tiles placed into a pool stretching 175 feet (53 meters) in length, floating just beneath the smooth reflective surface. The appearance at night is striking, as the crescent-shaped fountain illuminates from the edge, allowing the artwork to glow above a base of dark granite.

The Donor Fountain is framed by sculpted landforms, bluestone paving, and native plantings to help create a compelling, contemplative space for patients, visitors, and staff. Visitors can relax in areas surrounded by wildflowers, which bloom throughout the seasons; dine at the wheelchair-accessible tables; utilize the park's Wi-Fi capabilities; or simply spend time in contemplation in front of the Donor Fountain. Nearby, a granite dedication monument frames glass panels honoring Chlois G. Ingram.

The park design includes sustainable features, such as bio-retention cells to capture and purify rainwater from the surrounding streets and walkways, and LED lighting in the fountain. In addition, many of the existing trees were saved and stored during the construction process and then replanted as part of the final park. The new Spirit of Women Park provides a place of respite for patients, family members, visitors, and staff, and has proved to be a dramatic signature space for the Wexner Medical Center at the Ohio State University.

Master plan

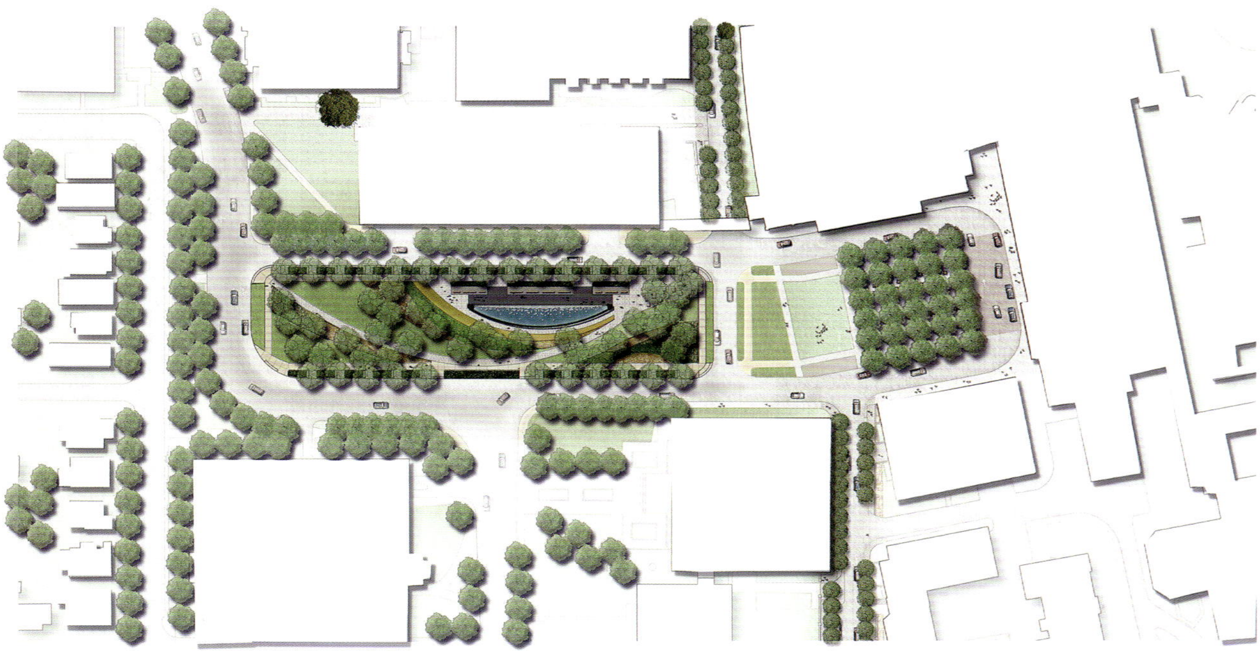

01

Artist's impressions

02

01 | Framed by native planting the main fountain offers dramatic views from the patient rooms looking out over the park
02 | Custom detailed infiltration basins, designed to seamlessly fit into the streetscape environment, capture and purify rainwater from the surrounding streets and walkways

The Ohio State University
Medical Center
03

sister
daughter
wife
aunt
Spirit Of Women Park
04

05

06

03 | The use of sculptural landforms and flowing pathways accent native plant massings
04 | Chlois G. Ingram's legacy, 'With a spirit of caring, compassion and kindness, the nourishment she shared healed hearts and restored hope' is inscribed on the monument in both the original and new parks
05 | A 95-inch (241-centimeter) stratified granite wall runs adjacent to an outdoor eating space, providing opportunities for informal seating
06 | A seating area, incorporated into the park design, adjacent to an existing café, provides opportunities for outdoor dining, and gathering

07 | Submerged recessed LED lighting, incorporated along the edge of the fountain, allows the artwork to glow at night
08 | Painstaking efforts were made to photo-document the original tiles, which were digitally recreated to match the original design; glass artists used a ceramic frit process to recreate each graphic on panels of glass, which were incorporated into the fountain
09 | The fountain design allows for water to spill along the main edge creating a soft noise in keeping with the quiet reflection of the pool
10 | The use of bluestone, granite, glass, wood, and native planting combine to form a rich tapestry of materials within the healing environment

HELEN O'NEILL SANFORD
1906
Mom, Kathy, Kathleen, Kellie
Natalie, Mary, Steph, Emma
Isla, Chelsea, Siobhan, Claire
Michele, Tina, Pam
Love, Bob
CAITLIN
Sue
Meridy
Jeni
Beth
Madeleine
Courtney
Cassandra
Carrie
Maya
08

09

11 | Every aspect of the park was meticulously thought out to include attractive and expansive space for patients, visitors, staff, and neighbors to relax in the area

12 | The fountain is framed by a perennial display throughout the seasons—yellow and white daffodils in the early spring, followed by purple iris, black-eyed Susans in the summer months, red rattlesnake master late summer, and the flowing grasses throughout use winter months

13 | All original donors were invited back to the Medical Center to dedicate the new Spirit of Women Park and reveal how their artwork had been transformed

14 | The park and fountain design reinforce the premise, 'To honor those special women in all of our lives', and hopefully touch the next generation

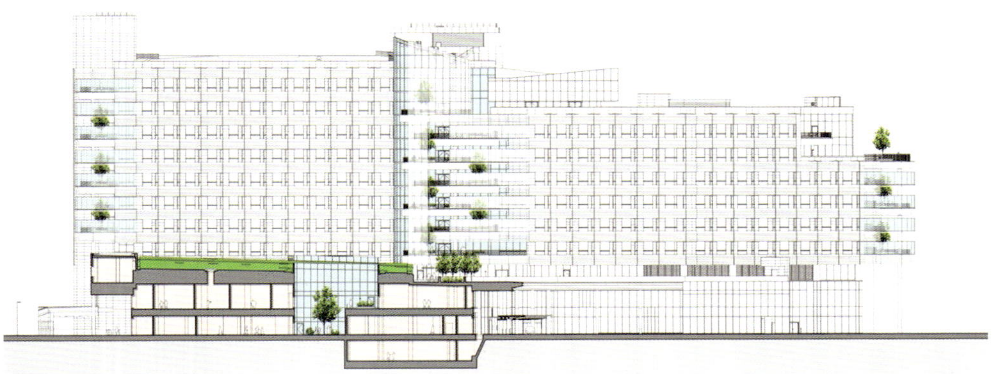

04 | On-structure café terrace

05 | On-structure gardens and amenities for staff, visitors, and patients

① Enterior courtyard
② Pre/post operation area
③ Emergency and imaging departments
④ Conference room
⑤ Waiting area
⑥ Mechanics
⑦ Support services
⑧ Loading dock

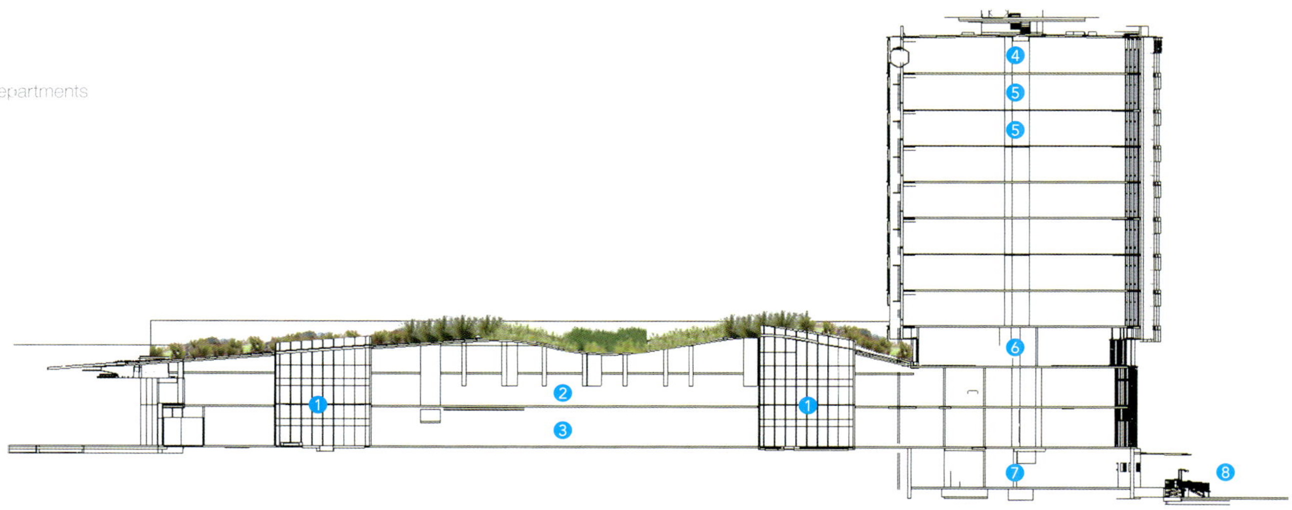

06

07

06 | Nursing-tower view terrace
07 | Green-roof native plants
08 | View of on-structure café terrace from tower garden

# Project Ripple

LOCATION
Miami, USA

CLIENT
Jackson South Community Hospital

COMPLETION DATE
2012

LANDSCAPE DESIGN
mikyoung kim design

PHOTOGRAPHY
Robin Hill

In the heart of Miami, Florida, this verdant healing garden offers respite from the daily activities of the Jackson South Community Hospital. The elements of stone, water, and earth feature alongside a rich palette of native plantings to create a healing space that encourages discovery and contemplation. The design is defined by the ripple concept which creates a sense of fluidity and is inspired by natural forms of sand and water. Layered landforms screen the perimeter of the garden, while the textured granite fountain serves as the garden's focal point. Mist emanates from the fountain, allowing users to interact with the fountain while lowering the temperature of the garden.

A strolling garden, framed by the planted berms and the central fountain space, offers opportunities for physical therapy in the garden. Contemplative seating areas are defined at the periphery, offering cool, shaded environments for smaller gatherings. The central space is designed to cater for intimate performances on the lawn.

The therapeutic garden, attached to the psychiatric unit, is a high-security area with a 12-foot (3.7-meter) surrounding barrier. The scale of the barrier is broken down with a graduated pattern, allowing the garden space to seem more open and inviting. Canopy trees and lush plant beds offer patients a pleasant, cool escape from Florida's summer heat.

BLUEPRINT

Master plan

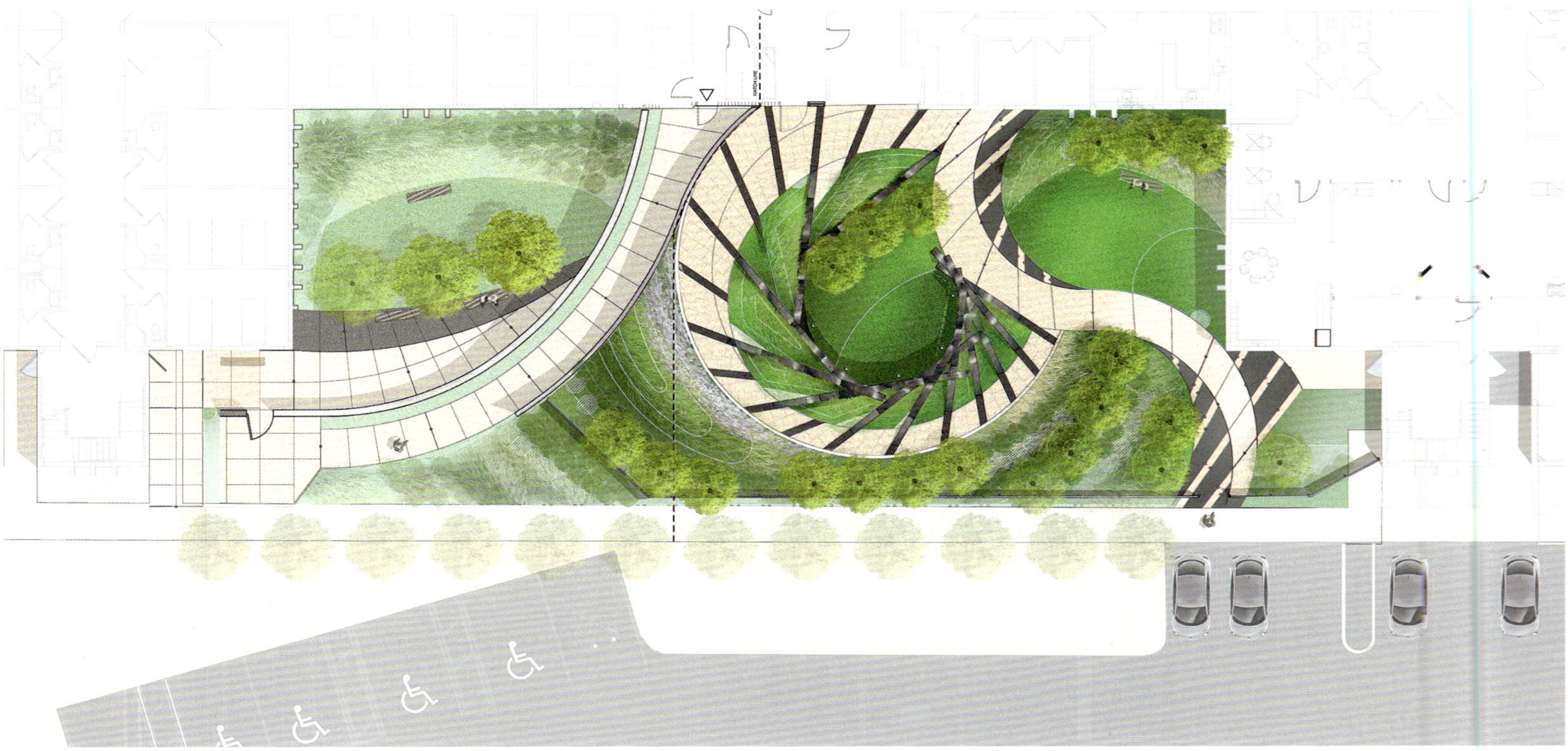

01 | Overview of the healing garden
02 | Mist in seating areas offering cooling and shaded microclimates for smaller gatherings
03 | The ripple garden during the evening

04–05 | Ripple concept creates a sense of fluidity, inspired by natural forms of sand and water

06–07 | Mist in seating areas during different times of day

# Military Hospital Garden

LOCATION
Berlin, Germany

AREA
28.42 acres (11.5 hectares)

CLIENT
The Federal Office for Building and Regional Planning

COMPLETION DATE
2014

LANDSCAPE DESIGN
Rainer Schmidt Landschaftsarchitekten GmbH

BUDGET
€3.34 million

PHOTOGRAPHY
Rainer Schmidt Landschaftsarchitekten GmbH

BLUEPRINT

As part of the redevelopment of the Federal Military Hospital in the district Berlin-Mitte, the entire landscape of the site was to be reshaped. The outdoor areas have technical functions such as delivery, but they are also places of relaxation for patients and staff members to unwind and stretch their legs. One of the open spaces, the patients' garden, is an example of the works carried out. The task was to encourage a more intensive use, to experience 'nature' in all its environmental and seasonal facets.

Old trees are combined with classic garden images to stir romantic memories of stately old villa gardens and inspire a feeling of security and safety. A central square connecting all entrances determines the development of the patients' garden. Framed by a horseshoe-shaped surrounding path laid with large, natural granite pavers, the courtyard garden ascends to the building's main entrance as a ramp—a very fashionable way to comply with accessibility requirements for disabled people.

An old stock of trees in the grounds was enhanced by planting delicately colored wild shrubs with plants flowering year-round. With its alternating rhythm of pavements and lawns, the garden is structured by 4-foot-tall (1.2-meter-tall) hedge elements, which creates a compartmentalized atmosphere and gives a wonderful range of views inside and out. The hedges have a shielding effect, ensuring privacy for visitors attending the garden.

As a reference to the historic courtyard, classical garden elements are reinterpreted and included in the redevelopment. The contemplative dimension—relaxation and recreation by stimulation and sensual perception of 'nature'—is an explicit feature of the gardens.

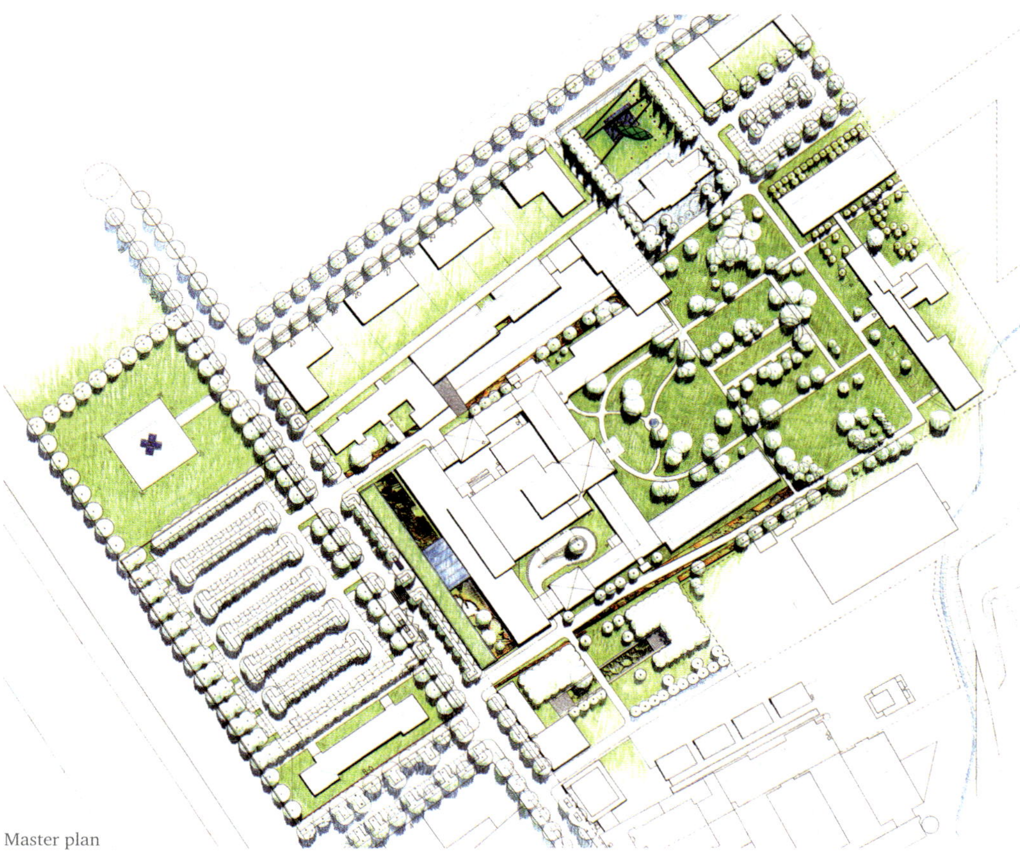

Master plan

01 | Patients' garden with view to the main building
02 | Accessible ramp that connects the garden and the main building
03 | Part of the horseshoe-shaped path with seating areas

Function area layout

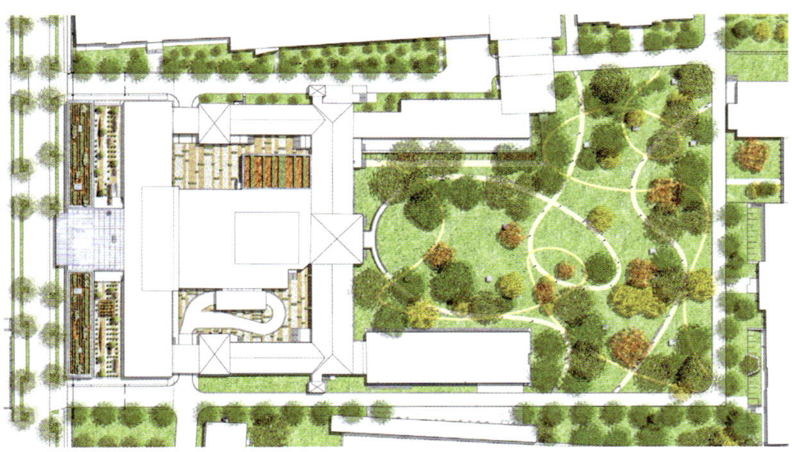

04 | The memorial stone in the garden of the hospital
05 | Climber plants, winding up the pavilion

06 | Pavilion with glass roof
07 | Flower bed with view of the main building and the memorial stone
08 | Detail of a bench situated under a pavilion

# Judge Fisher Senior Garden

LOCATION
Chicago, USA

AREA
1.2 acres (0.49 hectares)

CLIENT
Chicago Housing Authority, Harley Ellis Devereaux

COMPLETION DATE
2012

LANDSCAPE DESIGN
Site Design Group, Ltd

BUDGET
US$1.9 million

PHOTOGRAPHY
Site Design Group, Ltd

AWARDS
2012 American Society of Landscape Designers (ASLA) Illinois Chapter President's Award

BLUEPRINT

Judge Fisher Apartments, located in the Edgewater neighborhood in Chicago, is a Chicago Housing Authority Senior Housing facility retrofit project. Through research and discussions with residents the design team was able to develop a usable program for the residents while providing a therapeutic landscape that would allow residents to be closer to nature.

Prior to the project, the site was plagued with multiple problems. It had many accessibility issues, despite the fact that a majority of the residents have mobility problems. The main entrance did not meet current ADA standards; the parking lot was curbed and did not have accessible ramping; there was a curb cut alongside busy Broadway Avenue into the parking lot that created dangerous blind spots when entering or leaving; and, finally, the site did not allow occupants to freely move from the front of the building to the rear yard. The site also had a very unusual problem. A rare falcon had taken up residence atop the high-rise and was dropping its prey on the site below. This caused the apartment building managers to put up 'temporary' scaffolding as a permanent measure to shield debris from the bird's dinner falling on residents.

The new site consists of several loosely programmed areas instead of the typical public housing grass-and-sidewalk design. Programmed areas include a water feature that cascades into a rain garden, magnolia grove, trellis walk, 'lilac room', and community garden. The design addresses a number of existing accessibility issues and provides experiences for those with varying degrees of mobility. When discussing the project with building residents and property managers, it was noted that the seniors enjoyed strolling throughout the site and sitting to watch the neighborhood. Therefore, plenty of seating opportunities were incorporated into the design. Seating is provided by typical furnishings such as benches and picnic tables, but are also incorporated through grade changes and custom-built elements.

The entrance is flanked by a magnolia grove with benches and pedestrian bollard lighting. Residents are able to sit in front of the fragrant trees on custom-built concrete and benches. From the seating area in the lobby, residents are connected to the outdoors through views to a bubbling fountain that cascades down flagstones into a rain garden that captures the rain off a new roof canopy in large downpours. The canopy not only serves as a weather shelter, but also addresses the past concerns with the resident falcon. The entire element is built within seat walls.

The previously detached garden in the rear is now directly connected to the entryway gardens and the lush landscaping in front, allowing residents to walk entirely around the site. The picnic area, shaded by two mature trees, is now also home to different species of flowering lilac shrubs, and is appropriately named the 'lilac room'. The garden is in

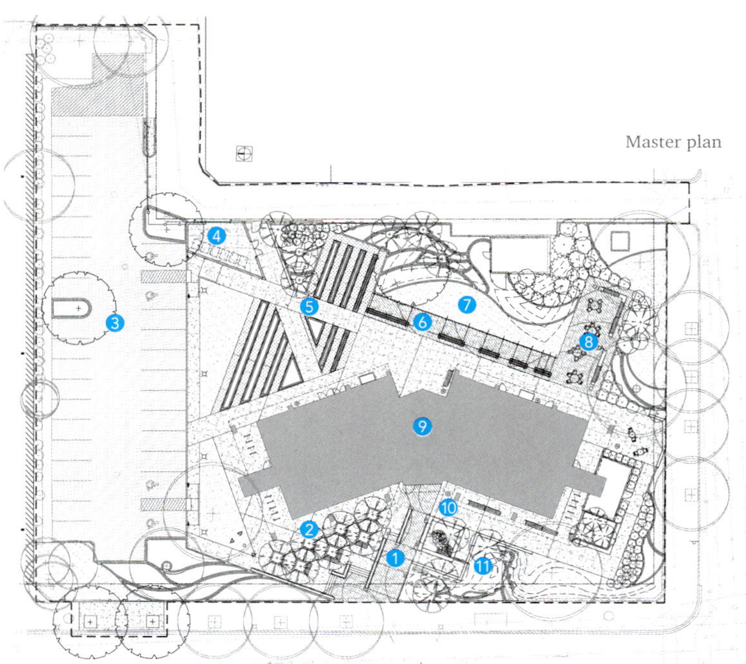

Master plan

① Entry planter
② Seating area
③ Parking lot
④ Trash enclosure
⑤ Community garden
⑥ Trellis walk
⑦ Lawn
⑧ Lilac room plaza
⑨ Judge Fisher apartments
⑩ Entry planter
⑪ Rain garden

bloom throughout the year providing a full sensory experience. Picnic tables, and backed and backless benches are located within the room for gathering and dining.

The 'trellis walk' is located alongside a sunny lawn and connects the lilac room to community gardens. The trellis walk features custom benches built into planters. The community garden planting area contains raised stainless-steel planters of different heights for those with different ranges of mobility, as well as built-in benches clad in wood.

This is the first Chicago public housing facility installation with an extensive landscape designed program. It will serve as a pilot project for the Chicago Housing Authority to determine the impact of innovative landscape design on the mental and physical health of its occupants.

01 | The spacing of posts on the trellis walk differs, to make the space seem longer.
02 | Flanked by seating on both sides, the trellis walk provides a path from the lilac room to the community gardens

03 | A tiered water feature is the focal point of the entrance; the three basalt columns bubble water from their tops, into a flagstone fountain, then onto a runnel that crosses a walkway, and finally into the rain garden

04 | Native and adaptive ornamental plants are adapted to the Chicago climate and change throughout the seasons

05 | Paying attention to even the utilitarian detailing, the trash enclosure was constructed using three different types of glazed CMU

06 | The 'lace' fence

07 | Residents use the entire site, sitting and looking at different elements within the garden and having conversations

08 | Surrounded by lilac shrubs and ornamental trees that bloom at different times, the lilac room is the most popular space during the spring

03 | Seating areas offer choices for socialization and privacy framed by native grasses
04 | Resilient, low-maintenance native plantings are incorporated throughout the medical campus
05 | Native trees provide shade and privacy in the staff lounge
06 | Lighting provides a welcoming and accommodating setting for evening use

# Nationwide Children's Hospital

LOCATION
Columbus, USA

AREA
6 acres (2.4 hectares)

CLIENT
Nationwide Children's Hospital

COMPLETION DATE
2012

LANDSCAPE DESIGN
MKSK/OLIN

BUDGET
US$10,695,000

PHOTOGRAPHY
Nick Fancher, Randall Schieber, Matthew Carbone

AWARDS
2013 American Planning Association-Ohio Planning Award for Focused Built Project
2012 American Society of Landscape Architects (ASLA) Ohio Chapter Merit Award
2012 American Society of Landscape Architects (ASLA) Indiana Chapter Merit Award

BLUEPRINT

When the acclaimed Nationwide Children's Hospital in Columbus, Ohio, expanded its campus with a new 12-story inpatient tower, the MKSK/OLIN team was brought in to design 6 acres (2.4 hectares) of green space, healing gardens, and urban park in the surrounding campus.

In collaboration with OLIN, MKSK developed the facilities master plan for the urban campus and was the prime consultant for the site infrastructure and improvements, leading a team of engineers, scientists, and designers. Green infrastructure practices were incorporated throughout the campus, including rainwater harvesting and a 2.5-acre (1-hectare) reduction in impervious surface. A 1-million gallon cistern captures all site and building rainwater runoff for use in irrigating the new park. Two acres (0.8 hectare) of the new green space is an intensive green roof over a subsurface parking garage. MKSK/OLIN worked with the parking consultant to verify loads and depths of engineered soils to support the shade tree plantings, bosques, and ornamental cherry promenade.

The design for the new hospital park serves the needs of patients, visiting family, and medical staff, while creating accessible space for surrounding neighborhoods. Within the park, a series of healing gardens offer a sensory-rich maze of plantings, including lemon and chocolate mints, wild thyme, fluffy lamb's ear, and colorful snapdragons, and are enjoyed by users of all ages and abilities. There's also a central, shady sitting area with playful seating elements, climbing mounds for children, outdoor chalkboards, an intimate storytelling area, and a moonlight garden. A luminous 'Grove of Light,' consisting of clustered illuminated beacons, defines the heart of the hospital campus. The design team created continuity between interior and exterior spaces to provide an enhanced visual and physical connection to natural materials and flora. This relationship is fully realized in the bluestone paved dining courtyard. Here, a tranquil area is bordered by grooved walls under a dappled canopy of locust trees and vertical plantings of Virginia creeper vine, creating a woodland feel.

Master plan

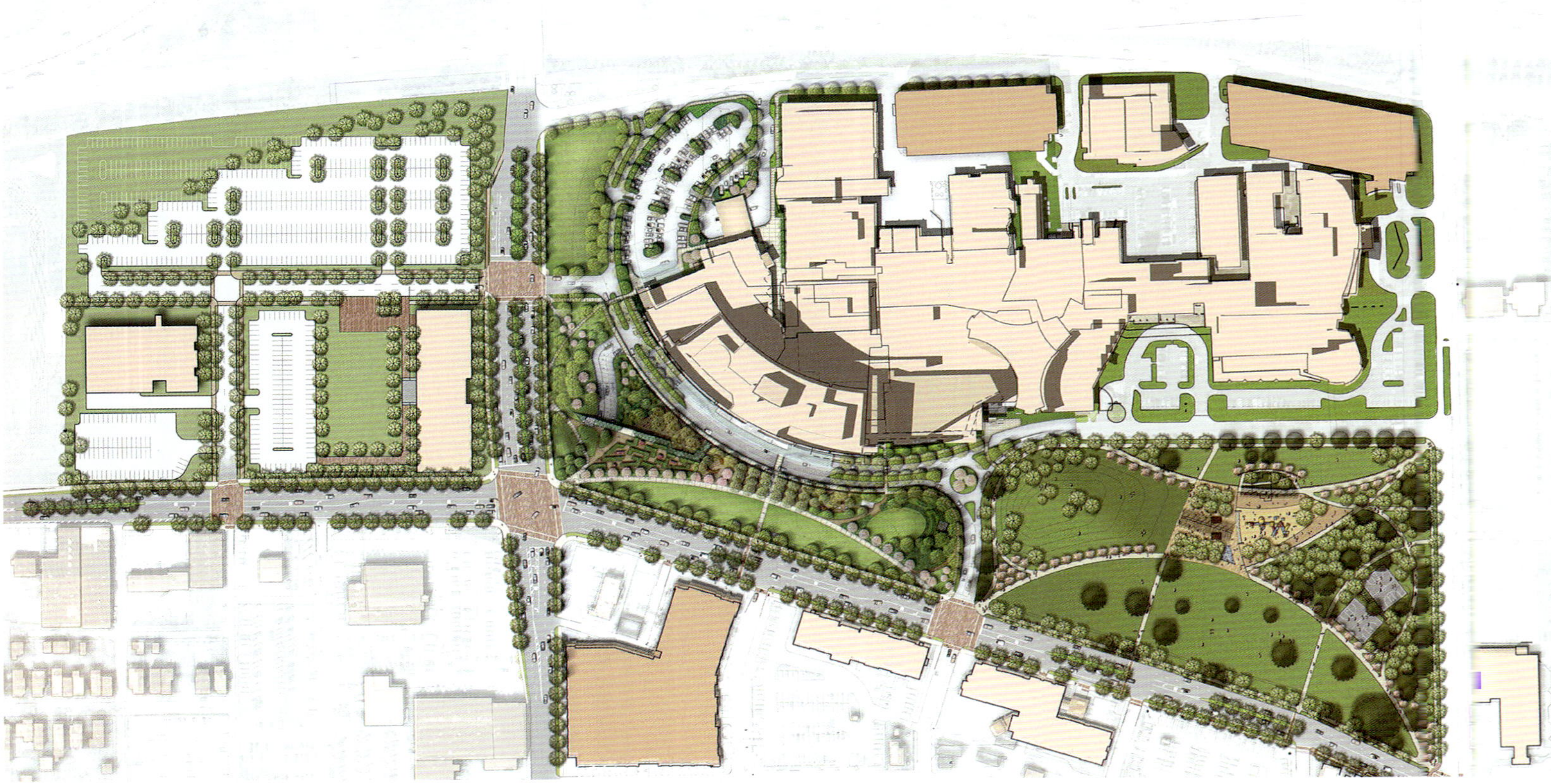

Section plan

01 | Children are the focal point of the medical district and healing gardens, which were designed to dynamically connect indoor and outdoor experiences

02

03

02 | District landmark signs demark the five entry points into the hospital
03 | Bluestone paving, textured concrete walls, a canopy of locust trees, and hanging catenary lanterns provide a tranquil respite in the dining courtyard
04 | In the evening, the playfully colored maze planters cast a softly glowing rainbow of light

05 | The serpentine benches appear to be growing from the playful mounds, creating a rhythmic landscape
06 | Surrounded by the lush plantings of the moonlight garden, 'mushroom' benches dot the lawn
07 | The combination of white and tri-color LEDs allows for a range of programmed lighting scenes from the illuminated masts

07

Perspective renderings

08 | The 'Grove of Light', a series of illuminated masts, defines the entry into the hospital

09 | One of the nation's leading pediatric hospital expands the principles of therapeutic gardens to the entire health-care campus and neighboring communities; additional streetscape improvements to the site include new pavement, street trees, and bio-retention cells for storm water runoff

# INDEX

## AECOM

P 64
Will Gabrielski, VP, Investor Relations
Phone / 213 593 8208
Website / www.aecom.com

AECOM's purpose is to create, enhance, and sustain the world's built, natural, and social environments. The company works with clients in more than 150 countries to design (including planning and engineering), build, finance, operate, and maintain diverse types of infrastructure.

## Brydges Landscape Architecture Inc.

P 90
35 Galt St. Guelph, Ontario, N1H 3G5, Canada
Phone / 519 766 1331
Website / www.brydgeslandscapearchitecture.com

Brydges Landscape Architecture Inc. was established in 2004 by Senior Landscape Architect, Paul R. Brydges. Paul brings over 25 years of combined design/build and construction experience to the design process. Corporate memberships include the OALA, ASLA, CSLA, Landscape Ontario and Green Roofs for Healthy Cities.

## C.F. Møller Architects

P 110
Europaplads 2, 11. 8000 Aarhus C, Denmark
Phone / +45 8730 5300
Website / www.cfmoller.com

C.F. Møller Architects is one of Scandinavia's oldest and largest architectural practices. Their award-winning work involves a wide range of expertise that covers all architectural services, landscape architecture, product design, health-care planning, and management advice on user consultation, change management, space planning, logistics, client consultancy, and organizational development.

## Cleve West

P 192
Navigator House, 60 High Street, Hampton Wick, Surrey KT1 4DB, UK
Phone / +44 (0) 20 8977 3522
Website / www.horatiosgarden.org.uk

Cleve runs an award-winning studio in Hampton Wick, southwest London, and has been designing gardens since 1990. Projects are diverse, ranging from contemporary urban spaces to large country estates mostly in the UK, occasionally abroad. These, in turn, vary in style according to the house and its surroundings, but essentially they are spaces that are both engaging and restful.

## Dekker Perich Sabatini

P 84
7601 Jefferson NE, Suite 100, Albuquerque, NM 87109
Phone / 505 761 9700
Website / www.dpsdesign.org

Dekker Perich Sabatini (D/P/S) has served clients for more than 50 years. The firm began as an offshoot of Art Dekker Architects, founded in 1959 in Albuquerque by the father of current principal Dale Dekker. They became D/P/S in 1998 with the merger of Dekker/Perich & Associates and Holmes/Sabatini & Associates. Since 1959, they have built a solid reputation for exceptional customer service and design excellence.

## Dirtworks Landscape Architecture, PC

PP 44, 68, 72, 120, 174, 180, 234
315 West 39th Street, Studio 910, New York, NY 10018, USA
Phone / 212 529 2263
Fax / 212 505 0904
Website / www.dirtworks.us

Dirtworks Landscape Architecture, PC was founded on the belief that excellence in design can heighten life's experiences, honoring both the site and the individual to offer opportunities to connect to the larger world.

## Fluidity Design Consultants

P 30
3780 Wilshire Blvd, Suite 230, Los Angeles, CA 90010, USA
Phone / 213 739 9291
Website / www.fluidity-design.com

Founded in 2002, Fluidity Design Consultants is a leading-edge, Los Angeles–based water-feature design and engineering firm with an international practice. Fluidity's work has been recognized for its creativity and design excellence by numerous awards, competition successes, publications, and speaking engagements. The firm collaborates with many of the world's most respected architects, landscape architects, planners, institutions, and developers in the realization of socially significant and exciting environments for many kinds of projects. The company is staffed by a team of architects, designers, and engineers, led by founding principal James Garland AIA, who participates in the development of all Fluidity's projects.

## Guillermo Vázquez Consuegra

PP 100
Dos de Mayo nº6 Sevilla 41001, Spain
Phone / 34 954 21 35 90
Website / www.vazquezconsuegra.com

## HOSPER

P 38
Kinderhuissingel 1d, Postbus 5231, 2000 CE Haarlem, The Netherlands
Phone / +31 (0)23 5317060
Website / www.hosper.nl

HOSPER works on a wide range of assignments, ranging from master plans to the design of outdoor furniture; in the city, on the urban periphery or further afield. A number of design disciplines are represented in the teams: landscape architecture, urban planning, architecture, and industrial design. This enables designs to be assessed straight away at a higher level of scale for their potential implications at lower levels of scale, and vice versa.

## INTERSTICE Architects

PP 60, 80
1173 Sutter Street, San Francisco, CA 94109, USA
Phone / 415 285 3960
Website / www.intersticearchitects.com

INTERSTICE was born as a multi-disciplinary firm of architects, landscape architects, urban designers, and visual artists. Over the past 15 years, this critical practice has grown, designing public and private spaces on projects of multiple scales, focused on the broadest possible interpretation of the constructed realm.

## Levi + Wong Design Associates, Inc.

P 94
45 Walden Street, Concord, MA 01742, USA
Phone / 978 371 1945
Website / www.lwda.com

Levi + Wong Design is a passionate group of professionals who believe the power of design can improve the quality of life in the communities where they live and work. Quality design, service, innovation, team work and sound business are the foundation of their success. They are a client-centric firm led by working principals dedicated to design excellence.

## McGregor Coxall Pty Ltd

P 152
Sydney Studio, 21C Whistler Street, Sydney 2095, Australia
Phone / +61 2 9977 3853
Website / mcgregorcoxall.com

McGregor Coxall are proponents of a new wave of environmentally focused landscape architecture, which is framed within a modernist design approach. Drawing on a diverse in-house team with expertise in landscape architecture, urban design, architecture, graphics, planning, horticulture, and urban ecology, they cross traditional design boundaries.

## mikyoung kim design

PP 50, 222
119 Braintree Street, Suite 103, Boston, MA 02134, USA
Phone / 617 782 9130
Website / myk-d.com

For the last 20 years, mikyoung kim design has crafted an exceptional body of work, spanning a wide range of landscape typologies in the United States, East Asia, and the Middle East. The firm has developed a reputation for culturally significant design work that serve as a powerful tool to heal and enliven the public realm. Their work addresses pressing environmental issues, while celebrating the beauty of their collective human experience through the use of contemporary materials and technologies. Today, mikyoung kim design's work is defined by a seasoned understanding of material detailing and a whimsical celebration of the transformative and healing power of the natural world.

## MKSK

P 138, 208, 238

462 S. Ludlow Alley, Columbus, Ohio 43215, USA
Phone / 614 621 2796
Website / www.mkskstudios.com

Established in 1990, MKSK is one of the largest landscape architecture, planning, and urban design firms in the Midwestern United States with offices in Columbus, Ohio; Covington and Lexington, Kentucky and Indianapolis, Indiana. MKSK offers clients innovative design solutions, state-of-the-art technical expertise, and the highest possible level of service and attention. With over 150 regional and national design awards, MKSK have been recognized by their peers as leaders in landscape architecture, land planning, and urban design services. MKSK is proud of projects that have truly transformed their communities. They seek to arrive at solutions that provide meaningful sustainable results: socially, environmentally and economically.

## Murray & Associates

P 78

16 The Seapoint Building, 44/45 Clontarf Road, Dublin 3, D03 RF63, Ireland
Phone / +353 (0)1 854 0090
Website / www.murray-associates.com

Murray & Associates is a leading landscape architecture practice based in Clontarf, Dublin. The practice was founded in 1991 and undertakes a wide range of projects within the sphere of landscape consultancy including landscape design, environmental planning, arboricultural survey and landscape management.

## NBBJ

P 186

523 W. 6th Street, Suite 300, Los Angeles, CA 90014, USA
Phone / +1 (213) 243 3333
Website / www.nbbj.com

Elevated street grids and floodable architecture could help Boston prepare for sea-level rise, proposed NBBJ in its award-winning submission for the Boston Living with Water competition. Invited by Fast Company to describe the workplace of the future, NBBJ predicts increased support for motion, technology, nature, mobility and choice—including ramped offices that allow people to cycle directly to their desks.

## Rainer Schmidt Landschaftsarchitekten GmbH

P 226

Von-der-Tann-Str. 7, 80539 München, Germany
Phone / 089 20 25 35 0
Website / www.rainerschmidt.com

Rainer Schmidt have been designing and implementing projects on different scales for 25 years in Germany and abroad, specializing in the regions of North Africa, Middle East, and Asia. The firm has three offices in Germany: the head office is in Munich; one branch office is in Berlin and the other in Bernburg.

## Rios Clementi Hale Studios

P 164

639 N. Larchmont Blvd, Suite 100, Los Angeles, CA 90004, USA
Phone / +323 785 1800
Website / www.rchstudios.com

Rios Clementi Hale Studios was founded in 1985 as a multi-disciplinary design firm. They create singular, integrated, and comprehensive solutions for a variety of design challenges. Their talents comprise a wide range of professional skills including architecture, landscape architecture, urban planning and design, interior design, graphics and signage, and exhibit and product design. Project types include commercial, residential, civic, educational, institutional, exhibits, and product and furniture design.

## RTKL

P 124

2101 L Street, NW, Suite 200, Washington, DC, 20037, USA
Phone / 202 833 4400
Website / www.rtkl.com

RTKL draws upon their global resources to provide clients with the most comprehensive set of end-to-end planning, architectural, and creative services available in the marketplace today. Always at their table: great architecture rooted in smart planning and urban design, but they take that model to the next level with services such as interior design and environmental graphic design, and intelligent engineering and applied technology services. In the end, they create fluid, cohesive, sustainable environments that serve the needs of today and stand the test of time.

## Sikora Wells Appel

PP 56, 170

8 Kings Highway West, Suite A, Haddonfield, NJ 08033, USA
Phone / 856 433 6380
Website / www.sikora-wa.com

Sikora Wells Appel is a landscape architecture and urban design studio that strives to create beautiful places that are socially and environmentally sustainable. Originally founded in 1979, the firm's approach is rooted in the synthesis of planning, the art of design and the science of ecology.

## Spurlock Poirier Landscape Architects

P 216

2122 Hancock Street San Diego, CA 92110, USA
Phone / 619 681 0090
Website / www.sp-land.com

For 25 years, Spurlock Poirier has nurtured a practice that creates transformative, restorative urban and natural landscapes that connect people, communities, and environments. They combine deep understanding of regional ecologies with critical analysis, research, and design rigor to shape places that make a difference.

## Studio Fink

P 144

154 Narrow Street, London E14 8BP, UK
Phone / 0044 (0) 2071 484 693
Website / www.studiofink.eu

Peter Fink was born in London and grew up in Czechoslovakia. The difficulties of obtaining art material and studio space, as well as the dominant ideology of art in the service of the state, led him initially to study engineering. Upon resettling in London in his early twenties, after the Russian invasion, he studied sculpture at St Martin's and later philosophy at UCL.

## Tales of the Earth

P 160

66 Millbrook Crescent, Toronto, Ontario M4K 1H4, Canada
Phone / 416 469 9646
Website / www.talesoftheearth.com

Inspired by sacred landscapes, Tales of the Earth has designed and built public and private gardens since 1984, with a special interest in landscapes for meditation and healing for residences, spiritual centres, health-care facilities and urban spaces. These gardens are grounded in design principles that help strengthen physical, mental, and spiritual health in a balanced and harmonious relationship with the natural and social environment.

## Yoshiki Toda Landscape & Architect Co., Ltd.

P 130

3F Miyuki Bldg 1-36-1, Yoyogi, Shibuya-ku, Tokyo, 151-0053, Japan
Phone / 81 3 3320 8601
Website / www.todafu.co.jp

Toda Fukei was founded by Toda Fukei who graduated from the Faculty of Landscape, Tokyo University of Agriculture, in 1970. After training as a gardener in Tokyo and Kyoto, he worked at Urban Design Consultant (headed by Kisho Kurokawa); then he established his own firm, Yoshiki Toda Landscape Design Office, in 1980, later renamed Yoshiki Toda Landscape and Architect Co. Ltd.

Published in Australia in 2016 by
The Images Publishing Group Pty Ltd
Shanghai Office
ABN 89 059 734 431
6 Bastow Place, Mulgrave, Victoria 3170, Australia
Tel: +61 3 9561 5544 Fax: +61 3 9561 4860
books@imagespublishing.com
www.imagespublishing.com


The Images Publishing Group Reference Number: 1204



Title: Healing Garden
Author: David Kamp (editor)
ISBN: 9781864706444 (hardback)

For Catalogue-in-Publication data, please see the National Library of Australia entry

Printed by Toppan Leefung Printing (Shenzhen) Co. Ltd / China